BIBLE BELIEVER'S ARCHAEOLOGY

VOLUME 3
BEHOLD THE MAN!
JOHN ARGUBRIGHT

Copyright © 2013 by John Argubright

Bible Believer's Archaeology Volume 3
Behold the Man
by John Argubright

Printed in the United States of America

ISBN: 978-0-9792148-5-1

All rights reserved. No part of this publication may be reproduced or transmitted in any form or by any means without written permission of the publisher.

Unless otherwise indicated, Bible quotations are taken from The Holy Bible, New King James Version. Copyright © 1962 by Thomas Nelson, Inc. Also quoted: New International Version Copyright © 1973, 1978, 1984 by International Bible Society. Copyright © 1986 Zondervan Publishing House

This book is copyrighted to protect its misuse and to safeguard the rights of any author, publisher, or individual whose data may have been used in research for this book and to preserve the integrity of quotes from historical sources.

The majority of the historical quotes used in this book were re-translated by the author in an effort to not infringe upon the copyright of others and to protect the authors and publishers of the original source translations.

This book as well as our first and second volumes in the series may be ordered at "BibleHistory.net" as well as from other major online book distributors.

FOUR THINGS GOD WANTS YOU TO KNOW

1. You are a sinner and cannot save yourself.

For all have sinned and fall short of the glory of God.
Romans 3:23

2. God loves and values you so much, He made a way for you to be saved. (Jesus)

"For God so loved the world that He gave His only begotten Son, that whoever believes in Him should not perish but have everlasting life." John 3:16

3. You must repent, Turn to Christ and turn away from your sins. Confess them and forsake them.

If we confess our sins, He is faithful and just to forgive us our sins and to cleanse us from all unrighteousness. 1 John 1:9

4. There is a Heaven and there is a Hell. Where will you spend your Eternity?

"He who believes in the Son has everlasting life; and he who does not believe the Son shall not see life, but the wrath of God abides on him." John 3:36

Introduction

The third book in the Bible Believer's Archaeology Series continues to provide some of the best evidences from archaeology and ancient history currently available to confirm the accuracy of the Bible.

Evidences are provided for Queen Esther and her uncle Mordecai, Herod Agrippa II and his sister Bernice, the Proconsul Sergius Paulus, the Plague of Boils on Egypt, the Exodus from the Pyramids, the earliest mention of the Hebrews, King Joash of Samaria, wicked king Menahem, Josiah's battle with pharaoh Necho, Tirhakah king of Ethiopia, Jeremiah chapter 39, and many others.

Ever hear people say that the Bible is just a bunch of made up stories? This book, as well as the other books in our series proves otherwise. Take a look and judge for yourself, you will be amazed as to what you find.

About the Author:

John Argubright is a researcher and author of the three volume series, *Bible Believer's Archaeology*, as well as the creator of the popular website, BibleHistory.net.

Table of Contents

KINGS FROM THE EAST SHALL BOW	Page 1
BY HIS STRIPES	Page 7
SERGIUS PAULUS	Page 12
THE SAMARITAN TEMPLE	Page 16
ACTS 17 - THE UNKNOWN GOD	Page 22
BERNICE AND HEROD AGRIPPA	Page 28
THE FINAL SCAPEGOAT IS CHOSEN	Page 34
EXODUS FROM THE PYRAMIDS	Page 37
THE PLAGUE OF BOILS ON EGYPT	Page 45
ISRAEL & THE HEBREWS	Page 50
JOASH KING OF SAMARIA	Page 56
MENAHEM	Page 60
TIRHAKAH KING OF ETHIOPIA	Page 66
JOSIAH'S BATTLE WITH NECHO	Page 76
JEREMIAH CHAPTER 39	Page 83
THE DANIEL SCROLL	Page 87
ESTHER AND MORDECAI	Page 92
SOURCES	Page 101

New Testament   Chapter 1

KINGS FROM THE EAST SHALL BOW

"Now after Jesus was born in Bethlehem of Judea in the days of Herod the king, behold, wise men from the East came to Jerusalem, saying, "Where is He who has been born King of the Jews? For we have seen His star in the East and have come to worship Him."

When Herod the king heard this, he was troubled, and all Jerusalem with him. And when he had gathered all the chief priests and scribes of the people together, he inquired of them where the Christ was to be born.

So they said to him, "In Bethlehem of Judea, for thus it is written by the prophet: 'But you, Bethlehem, in the land of Judah, Are not the least among the rulers of Judah; For out of you shall come a Ruler Who will shepherd My people Israel.'

"Then Herod, when he had secretly called the wise men, determined from them what time the star appeared. And he sent them to Bethlehem and said, "Go and search carefully for the young Child, and when you have found Him, bring back word to me, that I may come and worship Him also."

When they heard the king, they departed; and behold, the star which they had seen in the East went before them, till it came and stood over where the young Child was. When they saw the star, they rejoiced with exceedingly great joy. And when they had come into the house, they saw the young Child with Mary His mother, and fell down and worshiped Him. And when they had opened their treasures, they presented gifts to Him: gold, frankincense, and myrrh." Matthew 2:1-11

Two well known historians confirm that it was a commonly held belief amongst the Jews, as well as the people of the East, that a ruler would come forth from Judea.

The Roman historian Tacitus wrote: "[the Jews] firmly believed that their ancient Scriptures, quoted by their priests, contained a prophecy of how at a certain time, when the East was powerful, a ruler would come forth from Judea, and He would secure a universal empire."

(Tacitus, Histories 5.13)

Another early historian, Suetonius, penned the following words: "An old and well established belief was held all over the Orient, that one would arise from Judea who would establish a government over all men." (The Lives of the Caesars - Life of Vespasian 4.5)

Another even earlier text was uncovered which is known as 'The Testament of Judah', it was part of a collection of texts supposedly written by the twelve sons of Jacob known as 'The Testaments of the Twelve Patriarchs', but more likely seems to have been penned in the second century before Christ. Fragments of two of the Testaments have been found in the Dead Sea Scrolls, those of Levi and Naphtali. The 'Testament of Levi' was dated by the Oriental Institute at the University of Chicago using Carbon 14, and was dated between 100 and 200 B.C., well before the birth of Christ.

The 'Testament of Judah' reveals what type of Messiah the people were expecting and also foretold of a star that would arise in Israel which would accompany His coming.

It states: "There shall appear for you a star arising from Jacob in peace. And a man shall come forth who is my heir, like the sun of righteousness, walking amongst the sons of men in gentleness and righteousness, and there will be no sin found in him. And the heavens will rain down upon him the spirit as a blessing from the Holy One. And he will pour out the spirit of grace upon you. This is the shoot of the most high God; the water of life for all humanity. He will shine his light upon the scepter of my kingdom, and from your root will arise the shoot, and through it will stem forth the rod of righteousness for the nations, to judge and to save all who call upon the Lord."

(Testament of Judah 24.1-6)

And that star, which the wise men from the east followed, led them to Jesus, the ruler of all kings. And thus the following prophecies found in the Old Testament came to life:

"Arise, shine; For your light has come! And the glory of the LORD is risen upon you. For behold, the darkness shall cover the earth, And deep darkness the people; But the LORD will arise over you, And His glory will be seen upon you. The Gen-

tiles shall come to your light, And kings to the brightness of your rising. "Lift up your eyes all around, and see: They all gather together, they come to you; Your sons shall come from afar, And your daughters shall be nursed at your side. Then you shall see and become radiant, And your heart shall swell with joy; Because the abundance of the sea shall be turned to you, The wealth of the Gentiles shall come to you. **The multitude of camels shall cover your land, The dromedaries of Midian and Ephah; All those from Sheba shall come; They shall bring gold and incense, And they shall proclaim the praises of the LORD."**
Isaiah 60:1-6

"He shall have dominion also from sea to sea, And from the River to the ends of the earth. Those who dwell in the wilderness will bow before Him, And His enemies will lick the dust.
The kings of Tarshish and of the isles will bring presents; **The kings of Sheba and Seba will offer gifts.** Yes, all kings shall fall down before Him; All nations shall serve Him. For He will deliver the needy when he cries, The poor also, and him who has no helper. He will spare the poor and needy, And will save the souls of the needy. He will redeem their life from oppression and violence; And precious shall be their blood in His sight. And He shall live; And the **gold of Sheba will be given to Him** . . . His name shall endure forever; His name shall continue as long as the sun. And men shall be blessed in Him; All nations shall call Him blessed."
Psalm 72:8-17

(Note: Sheba, Midian, and Ephah are tribes of Arabia descended from Abraham's wife Keturah as mentioned in 1Chronicles 1:32)

THE GREATEST SONG TO BE SUNG ABOUT THE KINGS FROM THE EAST:

1. We three kings of Orient are:
   Bearing gifts we traverse afar-
   Field and fountain, moor and mountain
   Following yonder star.
   Chorus: O star of wonder, star of night,
   Star with royal beauty bright,
   Westward leading, still proceeding,
   Guide us to thy perfect light.

2. Born a King on Bethlehem's plain:
   Gold I bring to crown him again,
   King forever, ceasing never,
   Over us all to reign.
   Chorus: O star of wonder, star of night,
   Star with royal beauty bright,
   Westward leading, still proceeding,
   Guide us to thy perfect light.

3. Frankincense to offer have I,
   Incense owns a Deity nigh;
   Prayer and praising, all men raising,
   Worship Him, God on high.
   Chorus: O star of wonder, star of night,
   Star with royal beauty bright,
   Westward leading, still proceeding,
   Guide us to thy perfect light.

4. Myrrh is mine, its bitter perfume
   Breathes a life of gathering gloom-
   Sorr'wing, sighing, bleeding, dying,
   Sealed in the stone-cold tomb.
   Chorus: O star of wonder, star of night,
   Star with royal beauty bright,
   Westward leading, still proceeding,
   Guide us to thy perfect light.

5   Glorious now behold Him arise:
    King and God and Sacrifice;
    Alleluia, Alleluia!
    Earth to heav'n replies.
    Chorus: O star of wonder, star of night,
    Star with royal beauty bright,
    Westward leading, still proceeding,
    Guide us to thy perfect light.

New Testament Chapter 2

BY HIS STRIPES

Pilate said "But you have a custom that I should release someone to you at the Passover. Do you therefore want me to release to you the King of the Jews?"

Then they all cried again, saying, "Not this Man, but Barabbas!" Now Barabbas was a robber.

So then Pilate took Jesus and scourged Him. And the soldiers twisted a crown of thorns and put it on His head, and they put on Him a purple robe. Then they said, "Hail, King of the Jews!" And they struck Him with their hands.

Pilate then went out again, and said to them, "Behold, I am bringing Him out to you, that you may know that I find no fault in Him."

Then Jesus came out, wearing the crown of thorns and the purple robe. And Pilate said to them, "Behold the Man!"

Therefore, when the chief priests and officers saw Him, they cried out, saying, "Crucify Him, crucify Him!"

John 18:39-19:6

An example of the accuracy of this Gospel account can be shown in the customary practice of releasing one prisoner at the time of Passover as mentioned above as well as in Luke 23:17.

Historical records confirm that this was indeed a yearly event performed during Passover. The following Jewish writings from the Mishna, Pesahim 8:6 states: "They may sacrifice (a Passover lamb) for a man mourning the loss of his family, or for one that clears away a ruin; as well as for the one who has been **promised to be released from prison.**"

Another example of the Gospel's accuracy can be found in how the Romans scourged and crucified their enemies. The historian Josephus gives us a glimpse into this barbaric practice.

"Forcing themselves into every home, they slew its occupants; so the citizens fled along the narrow paths, and the soldiers butchered those that they caught, and no method of plunder was overlooked; they also caught many of the common people, and brought them before Florus, **whom he first punished with stripes, and then crucified.** The entire number of those that were killed that day, including women and children, (for they did not even spare tiny infants), was about 3,600. And what made this attack even worse was that Roman barbarism had reached to a new level of evil; for Florus did what no one had ever done before, that is, he had given orders that the men who were of equestrian nobility be **whipped and nailed to the cross before his council;** who, although they were by birth Jews, they were still looked upon as being Roman citizens." Jewish War, Book 2: chapter 14:9

The way in which Christ was treated and suffered during His trial was also not unusual for the culture during the times in which He walked the earth. History records that the surrounding nations mocked anyone who claimed they were a king of the Jews. The historian Philo mentions one such incident shortly after the time of Christ:

"Gaius Caesar gave Agrippa, king Herod's grandson, the third part of his family inheritance to rule over, which in the past was governed by his uncle Philip the tetrarch . . . (Agrippa went to Alexandria) . . . (But the men of Alexandria) were filled with an ancient and what I may call an inward hatred towards the Jews. They were furious at the thought of anyone becoming a king of the Jews . . . they spent much of their time insulting the king in the schools, and planning all sorts of deeds to ridicule him . . . There was a certain man named Carabbas, who was afflicted with a gentle form of mental illness which came upon him from time to time; this man spent most of his days and nights destitute along the roads being harassed by the youth of the city; . . . they drove this poor man against his wishes as far as the auditorium. There they set him up on a high place where everyone could see him. They then flattened out a papyrus leaf and put it on his head instead of a crown, and clothed the rest of his body with a mat as if with a royal cloak and instead of a scepter they put in his hand a small stick which they found lying by the roadside and gave it to him. And when he had been dressed and adorned to look like a king, the youth in the crowd took up sticks on their shoulders and stood at attention on each side of him pretending to be his bodyguards with spears. Then others came up and gave him a mock salute, while others came to him and pretended that they wished to consult with him concerning governmental affairs. Then a multitude of voices from the crowd yelled out the title Maris (Lord); which is the name by which they call the kings of Syria; for they knew that Agrippa was by birth a Syrian, and also that he governed over a great district of Syria."

If the nations could mock an earthly king in this manner, how much more would their hatred grow against the true King of the Jews?

Isaiah the prophet, in one of the Lord's prophecies concerning the coming of the Messiah, spoke of His suffering servant and described how He would be mocked and rejected by men.

"Behold, My Servant shall deal prudently; He shall be exalted and extolled and be very high.

Just as many were astonished at you, So His visage was marred more than any man, And His form more than the sons of men; So shall He sprinkle many nations. Kings shall shut their mouths at Him; For what had not been told them they shall see, And what they had not heard they shall consider.

Who has believed our report? And to whom has the arm of the LORD been revealed?

For He shall grow up before Him as a tender plant, And as a root out of dry ground. He has no form or comeliness; And when we see Him, There is no beauty that we should desire Him.

He is despised and rejected by men, A Man of sorrows and acquainted with grief. And we hid, as it were, our faces from Him; He was despised, and we did not esteem Him. Surely He has borne our griefs And carried our sorrows; Yet we esteemed Him stricken, Smitten by God, and afflicted.

But He was wounded for our transgressions, He was bruised for our iniquities; The chastisement for our peace was upon Him, And by His stripes we are healed.

All we like sheep have gone astray; We have turned, every one, to his own way; And the LORD has laid on Him the iniquity of us all.

He was oppressed and He was afflicted, Yet He opened not His mouth; He was led as a lamb to the slaughter, And as a sheep before its shearers is silent, So He opened not His mouth.

He was taken from prison and from judgment, And who will declare His generation? For He was cut off from the land of the living; For the transgressions of My people He was stricken.

And they made His grave with the wicked; But with the rich at His death, Because He had done no violence, Nor was any deceit in His mouth.

Yet it pleased the LORD to bruise Him; He has put Him to grief. When You make His soul an offering for sin, He shall see His seed, He shall prolong His days, And the pleasure of the LORD shall prosper in His hand.

He shall see the labor of His soul, and be satisfied. By His knowledge My righteous Servant shall justify many, For He shall bear their iniquities.

Therefore I will divide Him a portion with the great, And He shall divide the spoil with the strong, Because He poured out His soul unto death, And He was numbered with the transgressors, And He bore the sin of many, And made intercession for the transgressors.

Isaiah 52:13-53:12

SERGIUS PAULUS

When the apostle Paul went on his first missionary journey to Cyprus along with his faithful companions Barnabas and John Mark, he came face to face with the Roman governor of the Island whom he led to Christ. His name was Sergius Paulus.

A number of possible references to him have been found outside of the Bible.

Two of these discoveries are from the Island of Cyprus and were found by a veteran of the Civil war by the name of General Louis di Cesnola. He would later be named the first curator of the Metropolitan Museum in New York.

The first of these inscriptions was found at the city of Silo in 1877, just a short distance north of the city of Paphos mentioned by Luke in Acts 13:6, just before Paul's encounter with Sergius Paulus. The inscription mentions "the proconsul Paulus" and dates to around 54 A.D. during the reign of Claudius. It reads as follows:

"Apollonius to his father . . . consecrated this enclosure and monument according to his family's wishes . . . having filled the offices of clerk of the market, prefect, town-clerk, high priest, and having been in charge as manager of the records office. Erected on the 25th of the month Demarchexusius in the 13th year (of the reign of Claudius - 54 A.D.). He also altered the senate by means of assessors during the time of **the proconsul Paulus.**"

The second inscription is from Kythraia (Chytri), located in northern Cyprus, and makes reference to a "Quintus Sergius" whose last name is missing from the inscription but could possibly refer to Paulus. The inscription, found on a blue marble slab indicates that this man must have lived during the reign of either Claudius, Gaius, or Tiberius Caesar. One translation of the inscription which is located in the Metropolitan Museum reads:

"[CLAUD]IUS CAESAR SABASTOA
. . . [Q]UINTUS SER[GIUS PAULUS]"

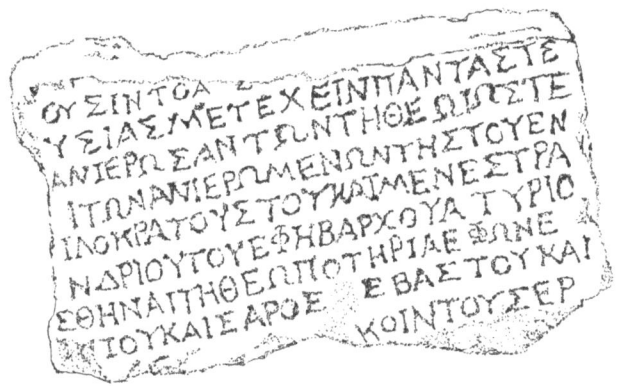

Quintus Sergius Paulus Inscription

Another artifact, a boundary stone set up by the Emperor Claudius Caesar was discovered in Rome during 1887 with the inscription "L. Sergius Paulus." His name was listed along with several others as being in charge of maintaining the banks and channels of the Tiber river. The inscription reads:
" . . . L. Sergius Paulus . . . curators of the river Tiberis . . . Claudius Caesar . . ."

The name L. Sergius Paulus was also found in 1912 on an inscription from Pisidian Antioch, a major military and administration base for the Romans in present day Turkey.

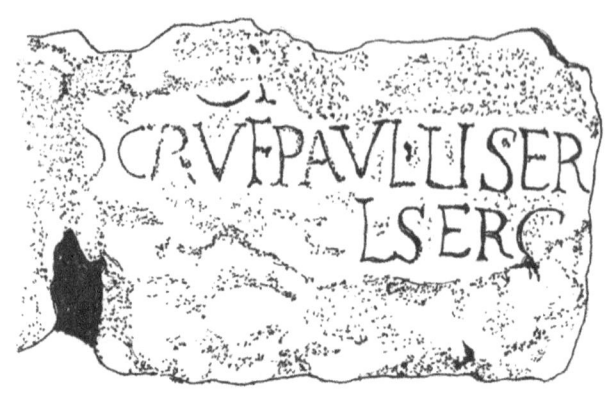

L. Sergius Paulus Inscription
Yalvac Museum, Pisidian, Antioch

The Roman writer Pliny the Elder also makes reference to a "Sergius Paulus" whom he used as a source along with others in Book 2 and 18 of his work on "Natural History." It is also interesting to note that Pliny mentions that the island of Cyprus was overrun with those who practiced sorcery, just like Elymas who the Bible says tried to deceive Sergius Paulus. Pliny writes: "There existed different groups of magicians from the time of Moses such as Jannes and Lotape, of whom the Jews had spoken of. And in fact many thousands yearly follow after Zoroastrian ways especially during recent times on the Island of Cyprus."

The story of Paul's first encounter with Sergius Paulus is found in Acts 13:6-12:
"Now when they had gone through the island to Paphos, they found a certain sorcerer, a false prophet, a Jew whose name was Bar-Jesus, who was with the proconsul, Sergius Paulus, an intelligent man. This man called for Barnabas and Saul and sought to hear the word of God.

But Elymas the sorcerer (for so his name is translated) withstood them, seeking to turn the proconsul away from the faith.

Then Saul, who also is called Paul, filled with the Holy Spirit, looked intently at him and said, "O full of all deceit and all fraud, you son of the devil, you enemy of all righteousness, will you not cease perverting the straight ways of the Lord? "And now, indeed, the hand of the Lord is upon you, and you shall be blind, not seeing the sun for a time." And immediately a dark mist fell on him, and he went around seeking someone to lead him by the hand. Then the proconsul believed, when he saw what had been done, being astonished at the teaching of the Lord."

THE SAMARITAN TEMPLE

While Jesus was traveling through Samaria, He stopped at the well of Jacob to rest from His journey. There He encountered a Samaritan woman who was about to find out what true worship was all about. She said to Jesus, "Our fathers worshiped on this mountain, but you Jews say the place to worship is in Jerusalem."

The mountain she was referring to was Mt. Gerizim, and archaeology has recently uncovered the remains of a temple complex up on this very mountain. You see the Samaritans built their own temple on that mountain many years earlier. And during the time it existed, they also had their own high priest carrying out all the duties found in the Old Testament books of Moses.

The story surrounding this Temple and how it came into being is a very fascinating one. The account is given to us by the historian Josephus. A summary of his account is as follows:

"During the time of Darius the third, king of Persia, a man by the name of Sanballat was sent by Darius to be a governor over Samaria. (This Sanballat was the grandson of "Sanballat the Horonite" who attempted to kill Nehemiah the prophet when he began to rebuild the walls of Jerusalem 100 years earlier.) Now Sanballat, wanting to live peacefully with the Jews, decided to give his daughter in marriage to one of the overseers of the Jews, a man by the name of Manasseh. He was serving in the temple in Jerusalem as a priest along with his brother Jaddua the high priest. (Jaddua is mentioned in the Bible's book of Nehemiah 12:11)

But because Manasseh married a woman who was not an Israelite, something the law prohibited, the Jewish leaders commanded him to either divorce Sanballat's daughter or stop serving in the Temple.

Manasseh, disturbed at this demand, tells his father-in-law the situation. Sanballat, not wishing to see his daughter divorced, promises to build a Temple on Mount Gerizim, where Manasseh would become the high priest. Sanballat also offers Manasseh a leadership position governing over the people of Samaria. In this fashion, Manasseh agreed not to divorce Sanballat's daughter, and this set into motion the wheels that began the construction of a temple in Samaria. But it was not by the command of God, but that of Sanballat himself.

During this time, Alexander the Great of Greece attacks Darius and defeats the Persian ruler. Alexander the Great sends a letter to the high priest in Jerusalem asking for supplies, and asking the Jews to break any ties they have with Darius. When they refuse, Alexander becomes furious and vows to march out and destroy the Jewish high priest.

On hearing of Darius defeat, Sanballat, along with a Samaritan army of around 8,000, decides to join forces with Alexander. He also asks Alexander for permission to build a Samaritan temple, telling Alexander that this would divide the Jews. Alexander agreed, and the new temple was built on mount Gerizim where Manasseh was made the Samaritan high priest.

Meanwhile, when Jaddua, the high priest in Jerusalem, heard that Alexander was coming, he ordered his people to pray and offer sacrifice to the God of Israel for protection. God later appeared to Jaddua in a dream and told him not to be afraid. He told him to decorate the city in wreaths, and as Alexander approached, the people were to go out and greet him dressed in white. The priests were to do likewise, dressed in their priestly robes. And God reassured him that no one would be harmed. On awaking from his dream, Jaddua rejoiced and spoke of all these things to the people.

Now it came to pass when Alexander advanced near the city, Jaddua went forth wearing the high priestly robes of blue and gold, along with all the other priests, dressed in linen, forming a long procession behind him. On Jaddua's head was placed a miter on which a golden plate was attached inscribed with the name of God.

On seeing this, Alexander dismounted from his horse and approached alone, prostrating himself before the high priest and greeting him. The rest of the Jews circled around Alexander and welcomed him.

But on seeing this, his soldiers pondered these things and thought that Alexander had gone crazy.

One of his officers went up and asked Alexander what was happening.

Alexander replied, "When I was at Dium in Macedonia, I pondered how I could conquer all of Asia. That night I saw this person, dressed as he is now, urging me to cross over immediately and defeat the Persians."

The high priest and his attendants then escorted Alexander into the city, there he was shown the Book of Daniel which predicted that a Greek ruler would arise to battle the Persians. Daniel chapter 11 verses 1-3 states: "Also in the first year of Darius the Mede, I, even I, stood up to confirm and strengthen him. "And now I will tell you the truth: Behold, three more kings will arise in Persia, and the fourth shall be far richer than them all; by his strength, through his riches, he shall stir up all against the realm of Greece. "Then a mighty king shall arise, who shall rule with great dominion, and do according to his will."

After hearing these words, Alexander realized he was the one of whom the prophecy spoke. He then offered the Jews whatever they wished. The high priest then requested that the Jews in Israel, as well as Babylon and Media, be allowed to live according to their own laws, to which Alexander agreed. Finally, he told them that if any would like to join his army, they could continue observing their own laws. And many Jews joined Alexander's army. The Samaritan troops from Shechem, located near Mount Gerizim, saw how Alexander had honored the Jews. So they claimed to be Jews as well and asked Alexander to visit their Temple. But Alexander declined the invitation. But during this time many Samaritans joined the Greek army as well."

    This reference by the historian Josephus to the Samaritans joining with the Greeks has some archaeological confirmation. A reference to the descendants of these very Samaritans, who worshiped on Mount Gerizim and who joined Alexander's army, was found on the Greek Island of Delos. The Samaritans seemed to have immigrated to this Mediterranean Island after serving in the Greek army. The inscription, which dates to between 250-175 B.C., states: **"The Israelites of Delos, who donate to the temple of Mt. Gerizim."**

    Now even though the other tribes of Israel looked down upon the Samaritans because they disobeyed God and intermarried with foreigners, the Samaritans referred to themselves as Israelites on the inscription, just as they had declared in the past to Alexander the Great.

    Roughly 200 years after the Samaritan temple was built, it would be destroyed by another Jewish high priest by the name of John Hycranus. Josephus accounts the following: "Hycranus now rebelled against the Macedonians (the Greeks) and no longer had dealings with them. He also decided to attack his nearby enemies, including the Samaritans.

    Hycranus attacked Mount Gerizim, destroying its temple there. And then marched against the city of Samaria. Having put the siege of the city under the command of his two sons, he left the battle. The Samaritans had assistance from the Syrians, but were finally defeated. Their city was laid to ruins and its residents were enslaved."

So at the time Jesus was speaking to the woman at Jacob's well, that very Samaritan temple was in ruins, sitting atop mount Gerizim. But she probably still went up on that mountain to worship God, because she thought the place was important. But Jesus told her, "Woman, believe Me, the hour is coming when you will neither on this mountain, nor in Jerusalem, worship the Father."

"You worship what you do not know; we know what we worship, for salvation is of the Jews.

"But the hour is coming, and now is, when the true worshipers will worship the Father in spirit and truth; for the Father is seeking such to worship Him.

"God is Spirit, and those who worship Him must worship in spirit and truth." John 4:21-24

Are you worshiping the Lord in Spirit and in Truth?

ACTS 17 - THE UNKNOWN GOD

"Then Paul stood in the midst of the Areopagus and said, "Men of Athens, I perceive that in all things you are very religious; "for as I was passing through and considering the objects of your worship, I even found an altar with this inscription: **"TO THE UNKNOWN GOD."**

Therefore, the One whom you worship without knowing, Him I proclaim to you: "God, who made the world and everything in it, since He is Lord of heaven and earth, does not dwell in temples made with hands. "Nor is He worshiped with men's hands, as though He needed anything, since He gives to all life, breath, and all things. "And He has made from one blood every nation of men to dwell on all the face of the earth, and has determined their preappointed times and the boundaries of their dwellings, "so that they should seek the Lord, in the hope that they might grope for Him and find Him, though He is not far from each one of us; **"for in Him we live and move and have our being, as also some of your own poets have said, 'For we are also His offspring.'**

"Therefore, since we are the offspring of God, we ought not to think that the Divine Nature is like gold or silver or stone, something shaped by art and man's devising. "Truly, these times of ignorance God overlooked, but now commands all men everywhere to repent, "because He has appointed a day on which He will judge the world in righteousness by the Man whom He has ordained. He has given assurance of this to all by raising Him from the dead." And when they heard of the resurrection of the dead, some mocked, while others said, "We will hear you again on this matter." So Paul departed from among them.

However, some men joined him and believed, among them Dionysius the Areopagite, a woman named Damaris, and others with them."

Acts 17:22-34

Altars have been found in both ancient Greece and Rome dedicated to unknown gods. For example, Rome gave orders to restore an altar, illustrated below, which must have fallen into a state of disrepair. The altar was not dedicated to any one particular Roman god as was the majority of their altars. The inscription reads: "Whether to a god or goddess / Sacred C Sextius/son of Praetor C.F. Calvinus/ by order of the senate/ has restored it"

Altar found on Palatine Hill in 1820 states: "Whether to a god or goddess."

Confirmation of these altars in Greece also come from two early writers, Pausanius in his account entitled "Description of Greece," as well as Philostratus in his work "Appolonius of Tyana." They both refer to "altars to an unknown god."

Paul also quoted to the Greeks two of their famous philosophers in order to point them to Christ, the true God. Their names were Aratus and Epimenides.

Aratus, in his work entitled "Phaenomena," stated: "Let us begin with Zeus (the Greeks believed Zeus was the top god), whom we mortals never leave unspoken. For every street, every marketplace is filled with Zeus. Even the sea and the harbors are full of his deity. Everywhere, everyone is indebted to Zeus. **For we are indeed his offspring**.

Phaenomena 1-5

You see, the apostle Paul was trying to convey to them that the unknown God was not Zeus, but the true God, Jesus Christ. The true God who created all things and every man.

The second philosopher Paul quoted was Epimenides, who stated in his work entitled "Cretica" the following:

"They fashioned a tomb for thee. O holy and high one . . . But thou art not dead, thou livest and abidest forever. For in thee we live and move and have our being."

Here Paul uses the poet's words to introduce the Greeks to the death and resurrection of the true God, Jesus Christ.

The historical account of Epimenides himself would also tie in nicely with presenting Christ to the Greeks for the first time. You see in the 6th century B.C., when the poet Epimenides lived, there was a plague which went throughout all Greece. The Greeks thought that they must have offended one of their gods, so they began offering sacrifices on altars to all their various false gods. When nothing worked, they figured there must be a God whom they didn't know about whom they must somehow appease. So Epimenides came up with a plan. He released hungry sheep into the countryside and instructed men to follow the sheep to see where they would lie down. He believed that since hungry sheep would not naturally lie down but continue to graze, if the sheep were to lie down it would be a sign from God that this place was sacred. At each spot, where the sheep tired and layed down, the Athenians built an altar and sacrificed the sheep on it. Afterward it is believed the plague stopped which they attributed to this unknown God accepting the sacrifice.

The Greek writer by the name of Diogenes Laurtius mentions these altars. He writes: "Altars may be found all over Attica which have no names inscribed upon them, which are left as memorials to this atonement."

THE UNKNOWN GOD IS MADE KNOWN

"No one has ever seen God, but God One and Only, who is at the Fathers side, **He has made him known to us."** John 1:18

THE MYSTERY IS MADE KNOWN

"Blessed be the God and Father of our Lord Jesus Christ, who has blessed us with every spiritual blessing in the heavenly places in Christ, just as He chose us in Him before the foundation of the world, that we should be holy and without blame before Him in love, having predestined us to adoption as sons by Jesus Christ to Himself, according to the good pleasure of His will, to the praise of the glory of His grace, by which He has made us accepted in the Beloved. In Him we have redemption through His blood, the forgiveness of sins, according to the riches of His grace which He made to abound toward us in all wisdom and prudence, **having made known to us the mystery of His will**, according to His good pleasure which He purposed in Himself, that in the dispensation of the fullness of the times He might gather together in one all things in Christ, both which are in heaven and which are on earth; in Him.

In Him also we have obtained an inheritance, being predestined according to the purpose of Him who works all things according to the counsel of His will, that we who first trusted in Christ should be to the praise of His glory. In Him you also trusted, after you heard the word of truth, the gospel of your salvation; in whom also, having believed, you were sealed with the Holy Spirit of promise, who is the guarantee of our inheritance until the redemption of the purchased possession, to the praise of His glory."

Ephesians 1:3-14

"Now to Him who is able to establish you according to my gospel and the preaching of Jesus Christ, according to the **revelation of the mystery kept secret since the world began but now has been made manifest, and by the prophetic Scriptures has been made known to all nations**, according to the commandment of the everlasting God, for obedience to the faith; to God, alone wise, be glory through Jesus Christ forever. Amen."

Romans 16:25-27

BERNICE AND HEROD AGRIPPA II

One of the apostle Paul's most eloquent presentations of the Gospel, along with his own personal testimony, occurs when he has an audience before King Agrippa and his sister Bernice.

An inscription found in Beirut mentions the following: "Queen Bernice and the great King A[grippa] in regards to King Herod, their great grandfather, who constructed the marbles as well as the six columns."

The Biblical story of Bernice and Agrippa is found in Acts 25-26:

"Now when Festus had come to the province, after three days he went up from Caesarea to Jerusalem. Then the high priest and the chief men of the Jews informed him against Paul; . . . And after some days **King Agrippa and Bernice came to Caesarea to greet Festus**. When they had been there many days, Festus laid Paul's case before the king, saying: "There is a certain man left a prisoner by Felix, about whom the chief priests and the elders of the Jews informed me, when I was in Jerusalem, asking for a judgment against him.

When the accusers stood up, they brought no accusation against him of such things as I supposed, but had some questions against him about their own religion and about a certain Jesus, who had died, whom Paul affirmed to be alive." . . .

Then Agrippa said to Festus, "I also would like to hear the man myself."

"Tomorrow," he said, "you shall hear him." So the next day, when Agrippa and Bernice had come with great pomp, and had entered the auditorium with the commanders and the prominent men of the city, at Festus' command Paul was brought in . . .

Then Agrippa said to Paul, "You are permitted to speak for yourself."

So Paul stretched out his hand and answered for himself:

"I think myself happy, King Agrippa, because today I shall answer for myself before you concerning all the things of which I am accused by the Jews, "especially because you are expert in all customs and questions which have to do with the Jews. "Therefore I beg you to hear me patiently. "My manner of life from my youth, which was spent from the beginning among my own nation at Jerusalem, all the Jews know. "They knew me from the first, if they were willing to testify, that according to the strictest sect of our religion I lived a Pharisee. "And now I stand and am judged for the hope of the promise made by God to our fathers. "To this promise our twelve tribes, earnestly serving God night and day, hope to attain. For this hope's sake, King Agrippa, I am accused by the Jews. "Why should it be thought incredible by you that God raises the dead?

"Indeed, I myself thought I must do many things contrary to the name of Jesus of Nazareth. "This I also did in Jerusalem, and many of the saints I shut up in prison, having received authority from the chief priests; and when they were put to death, I cast my vote against them. "And I punished them often in every synagogue and compelled them to blaspheme; and being exceedingly enraged against them, I persecuted them even to foreign cities.

"While thus occupied, as I journeyed to Damascus with authority and commission from the chief priests, "at midday, O king, along the road I saw a light from heaven, brighter than the sun, shining around me and those who journeyed with me. "And when we all had fallen to the ground, I heard a voice speaking to me and saying in the Hebrew language, 'Saul, Saul, why are you persecuting Me? It is hard for you to kick against the goads.'

"So I said, 'Who are You, Lord?'

And He said, 'I am Jesus, whom you are persecuting. 'But rise and stand on your feet; for I have appeared to you for this purpose, to make you a minister and a witness both of the things which you have seen and of the things which I will yet reveal to you. 'I will deliver you from the Jewish people, as well as from the Gentiles, to whom I now send you, 'to open their eyes, in order to turn them from darkness to light, and from the power of Satan to God, that they may receive forgiveness of sins and an inheritance among those who are sanctified by faith in Me.'

"Therefore, King Agrippa, I was not disobedient to the heavenly vision, "but declared first to those in Damascus and in Jerusalem, and throughout all the region of Judea, and then to the Gentiles, that they should repent, turn to God, and do works befitting repentance. "For these reasons the Jews seized me in the temple and tried to kill me. "Therefore, having obtained help from God, to this day I stand, witnessing both to small and great, **saying no other things than those which the prophets and Moses said would come; "that the Christ would suffer, that He would be the first to rise from the dead, and would proclaim light to the Jewish people and to the Gentiles**."

Now as he thus made his defense, Festus said with a loud voice, "Paul, you are beside yourself! Much learning is driving you mad!"

But he said, "I am not mad, most noble Festus, but speak the words of truth and reason. "For the king, before whom I also speak freely, knows these things; for I am convinced that none of these things escapes his attention, since this thing was not done in a corner. "King Agrippa, do you believe the prophets? I know that you do believe."

Then Agrippa said to Paul, "You almost persuade me to become a Christian."

And Paul said, "I would to God that not only you, but also all who hear me today, might become both almost and altogether such as I am, except for these chains."

PAUL PROCLAIMED THE SAME MESSAGE AS MOSES AND THE PROPHETS.

MOSES AND THE PROPHETS TAUGHT THAT CHRIST WOULD BE A LIGHT TO BOTH THE JEWS AND GENTILES.

"Rejoice, O Gentiles, with His people; For He will avenge the blood of His servants, And render vengeance to His adversaries; He will provide atonement for His land and His people." Deu 32:43

". . . In Galilee of the Gentiles. The people who walked in darkness Have seen a great light; Those who dwelt in the land of the shadow of death, Upon them a light has shined." Isaiah 9:1-2

"And in that day there shall be a Root of Jesse, Who shall stand as a banner to the people; For the Gentiles shall seek Him, And His resting place shall be glorious." Isaiah 11:10

"Behold! My Servant whom I uphold, My Elect One in whom My soul delights! I have put My Spirit upon Him; He will bring forth justice to the Gentiles."
Isaiah 42:1

THE PROPHETS TAUGHT THAT THE CHRIST WOULD BE CRUCIFIED.

"**My God, My God, why have You forsaken Me?** . . . But I am a worm, and no man; A reproach of men, and despised by the people. All those who see Me ridicule Me; They shoot out the lip, they shake the head, saying, "He trusted in the LORD, let

Him rescue Him; Let Him deliver Him, since He delights in Him!" . . . Many bulls have surrounded Me; Strong bulls of Bashan have encircled Me. They gape at Me with their mouths, Like a raging and roaring lion. I am poured out like water, And all My bones are out of joint; My heart is like wax; It has melted within Me. My strength is dried up like a potsherd, And My tongue clings to My jaws; You have brought Me to the dust of death. For dogs have surrounded Me; The congregation of the wicked has enclosed Me. **They pierced My hands and My feet**; I can count all My bones. They look and stare at Me. They divide My garments among them, And for My clothing they cast lots . . . Those who seek Him will praise the LORD." Psalm 22

THE PROPHETS TAUGHT THAT CHRIST WOULD BE RESURRECTED FROM THE DEAD.

"Your dead shall live; **Together with my dead body they shall arise.** Awake and sing, you who dwell in dust; For your dew is like the dew of herbs, And the earth shall cast out the dead." Isaiah 26:19

Old Testament — Chapter 7

THE FINAL SCAPEGOAT IS CHOSEN

In the Book of Leviticus, chapter 16, God instructed Moses and Aaron to select two goats every year for an offering. One was to be used as a sin offering to atone for the sins and transgressions of the people. Once killed, its blood was to be sprinkled on God's mercy seat on the Ark of the Covenant. There, God would view the blood of the sin offering and have Mercy on the people and forgive their sins.

The high priest would then lay hands on the second goat which was allowed to live, and he would confess the sins of the people, putting them on the head of the goat. The goat would then bear the blame for all the transgressions of the people and would be set free into the wilderness, where God would remember their sins no more. The goat became known as the scapegoat.

Jewish history records that it was a common practice to tie a red strip of cloth to the scapegoat. The red stripe represented the sin of the people which was atoned for by the red blood on the mercy seat. According to the Jewish Talmuds this red stripe would eventually turn white, signaling God's acceptance of the offering.

There is an amazing reference in the Talmuds that verifies that after Jesus was crucified, God no longer accepted the sin offering and the scapegoat offered by the high priests. The Talmuds state:

"Forty years before the Temple was destroyed (30 A.D.), the chosen lot was not picked with the right hand, **nor did the crimson stripe turn white**, nor did the westernmost light burn; **and the doors of the Temple's Holy Place swung open by themselves**, until Rabbi Yochanon ben Zakkai spoke saying: 'O most Holy Place, why have you become disturbed? I know full well that your destiny will be destruction, for the prophet Zechariah ben Iddo has already spoken regarding you saying: 'Open thy doors, O Lebanon, that the fire may devour the cedars' (Zechariah 11:1).'   Talmud Bavli, Yoma 39b

It's important to note that this event recorded in the Talmuds occurred 40 years before the destruction of the Temple, which was destroyed in 70 A.D. The date of this amazing event was 30 A.D., the same year that Jesus offered himself as a sacrifice on the cross.

Jesus was the final sin offering and the scapegoat bearing the sins for all mankind.

THE LAST SCAPEGOAT DIES ONCE FOR ALL:

But Christ came as High Priest . . . Not with the blood of goats and calves, but with His own blood He entered the Most Holy Place once for all, having obtained eternal redemption.

. . . And according to the law almost all things are purified with blood, and without shedding of blood there is no remission. . . . so Christ was offered once to bear the sins of many. To those who eagerly wait for Him He will appear a second time, apart from sin, for salvation. . . . For it is not possible that the blood of bulls and goats could take away sins . . .

By that will we have been sanctified through the offering of the body of Jesus Christ once for all . . . . this Man, after He had offered one sacrifice for sins forever, sat down at the right hand of God. . . . For by one offering He has perfected forever those who are being sanctified . . . says the LORD: I will put My laws into their hearts, and in their minds I will write them," then He adds, "Their sins and their lawless deeds I will remember no more."

Hebrews 9:11-10:17

THE RED STRIPE TURNS WHITE :

"Come now, and let us reason together," Says the LORD, "Though your sins are like scarlet, They shall be as white as snow; Though they are red like crimson, They shall be as wool.   Isaiah 1:18

EXODUS FROM THE PYRAMIDS

In a fascinating new book entitled "Exodus," by Garry Matheny, the author proposes a new site for the location of where Moses led the children of Israel out of Egypt. And a couple of very important landmarks still standing in Egypt today may mark where it all began. Those two landmarks being the Pyramids and the Sphinx located at Giza. And the Bible itself may just in fact mention both of them.

The main Biblical texts for the arguments are place names found in Exodus 12:37 & 13:18-14:9:

"Then the children of Israel journeyed from Rameses to Succoth . . . So God led the people around by the way of the wilderness of the Red Sea . . . So they took their journey from Succoth and camped in Etham at the edge of the wilderness. . . . Now the Lord spoke to Moses saying: "Speak to the children of Israel that they turn and camp before Pi Hahiroth, between Migdol and the sea, opposite Baal

Zephon; you shall camp before it by the sea." . . . So the Egyptians pursued them, all the horses and chariots of Pharaoh, his horseman and his army, and overtook them camping by the sea beside Pi-Hahiroth, before Baal Zephon."

Matheny first of all believes that the royal Egyptian palace to which Moses confronted Pharaoh was at Memphis, just seven and a half miles south of the pyramids at Giza. This is based on comments from early historians such as Philo, who when commenting on the seventh plague said: "the country beyond Memphis, where the palace of the king is." A position also held by the church historian Eusebius.

One of the candidates for the Exodus pharaoh, Thutmose I, also built a royal palace at the city of Memphis. A later pharaoh, Tutankhamun, mentioned he was residing at this "palace which is in the house of Thutmose I," which an inscription from the reign of King Tuts' successor, Pharaoh Ay, mentioned as being located at Memphis.

Exodus 12:37 tells us the place where the Exodus began. It was Rameses, which most scholars identify with the city of Avaris. This site was later incorporated into the city of Pi-Ramesses.

From there many different Exodus routes and sea crossing locations have been proposed. Some believe that God parted the waters at lake Ballah, others at the northern tip of the gulf of Suez, and still others at the Gulf of Aqabah.

But Matheny does not hold that the Israelites left from this site. He contends that the mention of Rameses was not the city of Rameses, but the broader area known as the "land of Rameses." To the Egyptians, Rameses meant the land which the Egyptian god "Ra created."

The "land of Rameses" was first mentioned in Genesis 47:11 which states: "Joseph settled his father and his brothers, and gave them a possession in the land of Egypt, in the best of the land, in the land of Rameses." Matheny speculates that this may have included all of the fertile lands in the Nile delta around Memphis. The Egyptians called the fertile lands the "Black Land" and the desert the "Red Land." And although he didn't provide any specific evidence crucial in proving his theory, the city of Heliopolis, which was the next major Egyptian city located just to the northeast of pyramids, was a major worship center for the god Ra. The Septuagint also adds Heliopolis to the cities of Rameses and Pithom which were built by the Hebrews according to Exodus 1:11.

The next location mentioned in Exodus 13:20 is Succoth, which Matheny identifies as Saqqara which overlook's nearby Memphis. Saqqara is a site where several kings were buried along with a number of Pyramids that were built there. Matheny contends that this would have been the royal burial spot of Joseph, whose bones were taken by Moses when Israel leaves Succoth as recorded in Exodus 13:19.

The next stop on their journey is Etham, "a place in the desert" at the end of the wilderness. And indeed Egyptian records indicate that traveling northward from Memphis towards the Pyramids at Giza definitely would describe this landscape.

The next place Israel stops is at Pi-Hahiroth near the Sea. Pi-Hahiroth's Hebrew meaning is "mouth of the gorges." And Matheny contends that this is the location of where the upper delta dumps into the mouth of the Nile river. This area regularly flooded and became as a sea. Matheny quotes from the historian Herodotus who states that the channels in the upper delta became flooded and boats could sail across it just as sailing across a sea.

Herodotus states: "They pass by the water not now by the channels of the river but over the midst of the plain; for example as one sails from Naucratis to Memphis the passage is then close by the Pyramids, whereas the usual passage is not the same."

This is where Matheny contends Israel crosses through the Red Sea. The Hebrew word translated Red Sea in the book of Exodus is ("cuwph"), meaning a reed, especially a papyrus, flag, or weed. And ("Yam"), meaning a large body of water or river. In other words, the reed sea. And this would indeed describe this flooded location.

In Exodus 14:2 it sates this location was between the sea and Migdol. The word Migdol means "tower" and is the same Hebrew word used in Genesis 11:4 for the "Tower" of Babel, the stepped Ziggurats of the Chaldeans. So Migdol would definitely be the appropriate Hebrew term the Israelites would have used when referring to the Pyramids.

According to Exodus 14:2 this site was also close by Baal Zephon which Matheny says means "The Lord of the North." Lord meaning a false idol or god. Baal Zephon was a god that was worshiped as far North as Syria, but was also attested to by the Egyptians through individuals traveling on errands of diplomacy and trade. Matheny believes Baal Zephon was known for being the protector god of mariners since the Sphinx was located at the apex of the Delta. There, all shipping on the branches of the Nile would pass, and mariners would have viewed the Sphinx as the god protector of the Nile.

Our own research indicates that the Hebrew word "Ba'al Tsephown" may also refer to the "Lord of Destruction," since Tsephown is a form of "Typhon" meaning "Destroyer."

And the Egyptians did worship a false goddess known as Sekhmet, who was known as the lion goddess of destruction, disease, plague, pestilence, and war. She was also known as the fierce protector of pharaoh. She had the face of a lion and the body of a woman. Interestingly, the Sphinx is somewhat similar, but just the opposite, it has the body of a lion and face of a man. The Pharaoh's also believed they were the children of Sekhmet. The Hebrews therefore may have associated the Sphinx with Sekhmet because she was the lion goddess and protector of pharaoh. Whether or not this is the case is uncertain, but it is interesting speculation anyhow. Interesting because of this false god being viewed as a destroyer and associated with plagues. Sekhmet was also associated with a festival dealing with when the Nile ran blood red from silt during flooding, which is very interesting as well.

If so, God was performing His signs and plagues right under the very nose of the Egyptian false god who was supposed to be able to protect pharaoh. God was letting Pharaoh know that his god was nothing before Him.

The Egyptian record below may also support the connection between Sekhmet and the Sphinx:

"Runner, racer, courser! **Khepri (Sphinx)** whose birth was distinct, whose beauty was upraised in the body of the **sky goddess** (Sekhmet was also a solar deity of the sky who sometimes is called the daughter of the sun God Ra.) He who illuminates the Two Lands with his (sun) disc, the primordial one of the two lands. . . . The sole lord who reaches the ends of the lands every day, being one who sees them tread thereon. ANET 368

The following Egyptian records also seem to support that Memphis, along with the area around the Sphinx and Pyramids, were important Egyptian centers at this time, as well as the fact that the Egyptians did worship the Sphinx as a god.

The first inscription, from the reign of Thutmose I, who may have been the Exodus Pharaoh, was found on a monument near the Sphinx. It mentions Amenmose, who was the first born son of Thutmose I. It reads: "In the fourth year of his majesty Thutmose I, beloved of **Harmakhis (the Sphinx)** . . . The eldest king's son, commander in chief of his father's army, Amenmose . . . went for a pleasure walk."

Another inscription found on the Sphinx itself from a later pharaoh, Thutmose IV, states:
"Now he used to occupy himself with sport on the **desert highland of Memphis**, on it's southern and northern sides, shooting at a target of copper, hunting lions and beasts in the desert, making excursions in his chariot . . . Now when his hour came for taking a rest . . . he paused at the ruins of **Harmakhis (area of the Sphinx)**, Besides Sokar in **Giza**; . . . Lady of the Southern Wall; **Sekhmet**, Presiding over Khas; and Hike, the first born of the holy place of primeval times; near the **Lords of Babylon (Egyptian Babylon on the east bank opposite Giza)**, the divine way of the gods to the horizon west of Heliopolis. Now at the very great statue of **Khepri (Sphinx)** rests in this place, great fame, majestic in awe, upon which the favor of **Re** rests. The villages of **Memphis** and of every other town which is beside it come to it, with their arms (outstretched) in **praise before it, bearing great oblations** to its ka."

"One of these days it happened that the King's son Thutmose came on an excursion at noon time.

Then he rested in the shadow of this great **god** . . . They shall protect the **offerings of this god** that they shall bring to him, . . . **Khepri (Sphinx)** in the horizon west of Heliopolis." ANET 449

Another inscription from Amenhotep II states: "Let there be given to him the very best horses in my **majesty's stable which is in Memphis**" . . . He would harness with the bit in **Memphis** and stop at the rest house in **Harmakhkis** (area of the Sphinx), so that he might spend a moment there, going around and around it and seeing the rest house at Khufu and Khaf-Re . . . After this, when his majesty was made to appear as king, the uraeus serpent, took her place on his brow, the image of **Re** was established at its post, and the land was in the first state, at peace under their lord, Aa-khepru-Re. He ruled the Two Lands and every foreign country was bound under his soles. Then his majesty remembered the place where he had enjoyed himself in the vicinity of the **pyramids and of Harmakhis**, and one ordered that it be caused that a rest house be made there, in which was set up a limestone stela, the face of which was engraved with the great name of Aa-Khepru-Re, beloved of **Harmakhis."** ANET 244

This last inscription also mentions that Memphis is the spot where pharaoh's royal stables were located. This may also verify where Pharaoh may have begun his pursuit of the Israelites as recorded in Exodus 14:6-8 which states: "So he made ready his chariot and took his people with him. Also he took six hundred choice chariots of Egypt with captains over each one of them . . . And he pursued the children of Israel . . ."

Of course Pharaoh and his armies would soon be destroyed by the God of Israel who would protect his people.

What the Bible says about people who worship idols like the Sphinx and the false religious systems of this world:

"Rather, that the things which the Gentiles sacrifice they sacrifice to demons and not to God, and I do not want you to have fellowship with demons." 1 Corinthians 10:20

"For they themselves declare concerning us what manner of entry we had to you, and how you turned to God from idols to serve the living and true God, and to wait for His Son from heaven, whom He raised from the dead, even Jesus who delivers us from the wrath to come." 1 Thessalonians 1:9-10

THE PLAGUE OF BOILS ON EGYPT

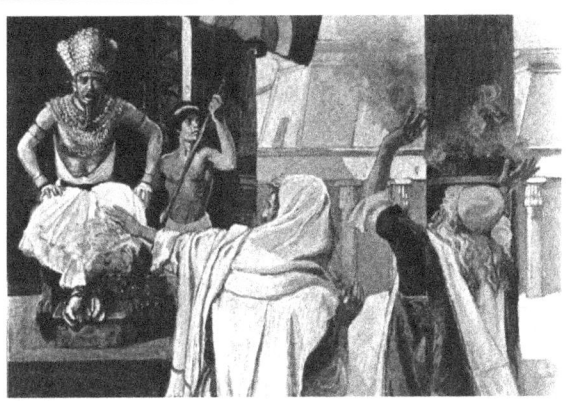

Evidence for the plague of boils which God brought upon Egypt may have come to light. In 2009, a fellow researcher, Ed Kaspar, wrote an article in which he proposed that the Exodus Pharaoh was Thutmose II. This is based upon recent CAT scans of the pharaoh's mummy as well as quotes from the original archaeologists that examined the mummy back in 1886 and 1912. The examinations and CAT scans revealed that Thutmose II had scarring on his flesh which may have come from a skin disease consistent with that of boils. Other mummies of individuals who were alive at the same time as Thutmose II were also found to have this same scaring. Those mummies included his wife Queen Hatshepsut, her wet nurse Sitre-In, and her stepson Thutmose III.

One Biblical timeline when matched up against one commonly used Egyptian Pharaoh timeline also has the Exodus falling on a date very close to the death of Thutmose II.

If Thutmose II was in fact the Pharaoh of the Exodus, there are some very interesting coincidences to support this. For example one common Egyptian timeline has Thutmose II dying in 1486 B.C., this would therefore be considered the date of the Exodus. According to the Bible, Moses was 80 years old at that time. Adding 80 Biblical years to 1486 B.C. would give the date of his birth. (Note a Biblical year is based upon a 360 day calender year not 365 days. So 1486 + (80 years x 360/365) = 1565 B.C., the date of Moses birth. The most likely candidate for Pharaoh at this time was a man named Seqenenre Tao. What is interesting about him is that all of his children's names, both sons and daughters, were comprised of the name "mose." Their names were Ahmose, Kamose, Ahmose-Nefertari, Ahmose-Henuttamehu, Ahmose-Sipair, Ahmose-Henutemipet, Ahmose-Meritamon, Ahmose-Nebetta, and Ahmose-Tumerisy.

    Many historians also believe that Seqenenre Tao was the one who began a war against the foreigners known as the "Hyksos" in the land of Egypt. This could tie in with the pharaoh's decree to kill Israel's newborn who were considered foreigners in their land. If in fact he was the pharaoh at the time of Moses birth, one his daughters would have been the one who had Moses pulled from the water.

Seqenenre Tao did have a daughter named Tumerisy who may in fact be the one who adopted Moses. The reason being is that two historians mention the name of pharaohs' daughter and they are similar to that of Tumerisy. The Jewish historian Josephus called her Thermuthis and the church historian Eusebius, quoting from Artapanus in his book "Concerning the Jews," says the daughter of Pharaoh was named "Merris." **Merris** a shortened form of the name "Tu-**Meris**-y."

If the Exodus occurred in 1486 B.C. then Moses would have likely fled from pharaoh "Amenhotep I" after killing an Egyptian forty years earlier in 1526 B.C. Another interesting coincidence is that during the reigns of Amenhotep and his predecessor Ahmose I, wars were conducted against Kush, better known as Ethiopia. This is interesting because according to Josephus, Moses took part in a military campaign against the Ethiopians before fleeing Egypt. And according to Josephus, that is when Moses met his Ethiopian wife.

Some question as to whether or not Thutmose II could have been the Exodus pharaoh because he would have had to have a son that perished in the plague on the firstborn of Egypt. To date there is only one known son of Thutmose II, who was Thutmose III. He ruled as pharaoh after him. So unless Thutmose II had another son who died in the plague of the firstborn, it would eliminate him from being the Exodus pharaoh.

The other possible candidate for the Exodus pharaoh would be his father, Thutmose I. His firstborn son, Amenmose, who was also put in charge of the Egyptian army under Thutmose I, did die before the death of his father. Possibly during the plague of the firstborn which led pharaoh to expel the Israelites from Egypt.

But since Thutmose II along with his wife Hatshepsut and his son Thutmose III were all alive during the reign of Thutmose I, they would have in fact witnessed the Exodus firsthand. And their mummies may indeed bare the marks of the boil plague which God brought against Egypt.

Mummy of Thutmose II

MOSES GAVE THE LAW
JESUS FULFILLED THE LAW:

"Do not think that I came to destroy the Law or the Prophets. I did not come to destroy but to fulfill. "For assuredly, I say to you, till heaven and earth pass away, one jot or one tittle will by no means pass from the law till all is fulfilled. "Whoever therefore breaks one of the least of these commandments, and teaches men so, shall be called least in the kingdom of heaven; but whoever does and teaches them, he shall be called great in the kingdom of heaven.
Matthew 5:17-19

Righteousness does not come by keeping the Law, Jesus declares righteous those who have been crucified with Christ:

"For I through the law died to the law that I might live to God. "I have been crucified with Christ;

it is no longer I who live, but Christ lives in me; and the life which I now live in the flesh I live by faith in the Son of God, who loved me and gave Himself for me. "I do not set aside the grace of God; for if righteousness comes through the law, then Christ died in vain." Galatians 2:19-21

THE JUST SHALL LIVE BY FAITH

For as many as are of the works of the law are under the curse; for it is written, "Cursed is everyone who does not continue in all things which are written in the book of the law, to do them." But that no one is justified by the law in the sight of God is evident, for "the just shall live by faith."

Yet the law is not of faith, but "the man who does them shall live by them." Christ has redeemed us from the curse of the law, having become a curse for us (for it is written, "Cursed is everyone who hangs on a tree"), that the blessing of Abraham might come upon the Gentiles in Christ Jesus, that we might receive the promise of the Spirit through faith. . . . Therefore the law was our tutor to bring us to Christ, that we might be justified by faith. But after faith has come, we are no longer under a tutor. For you are all sons of God through faith in Christ Jesus." Galatians 3:10-26

REDEEMED FROM THE LAW

"But when the fullness of the time had come, God sent forth His Son, born of a woman, born under the law, to redeem those who were under the law, that we might receive the adoption as sons. And because you are sons, God has sent forth the Spirit of His Son into your hearts, crying out, "Abba, Father!" Galatians 4:4-6

ISRAEL & THE HEBREWS

In 1896 an artifact inscribed with one of the oldest known references to the land of Israel was discovered in Egypt.

The inscription is dated to approximately 1210 B.C. during the Biblical period of the Judges. It records victories achieved by the Egyptian pharaoh Merneptah over the peoples in neighboring lands. It reads:

"The princes are prostrate saying: "Mercy! Not one of the nine bows (my enemies) lifts his head; Tjehenu is vanquished, Hatti is pacified, **Canaan is captive**, Ashkelon is carried away, Gezer is seized, Yanoam is made nonexistent; **the foreign people of Israel are laid waste**, bare of seed."

Merneptah Stele Inscription
"Israel - the foreign people"

The inscription also mentions the land known as **Canaan**, the land in which God had brought the Israelites into.

Of course typical of a proud Egyptian ruler, Merneptah exaggerated his victory over the Hebrews since Israel would later become a powerful nation under God's protection.

Although it is technically true that this is the first reference to "Israel" outside of the Bible, there are earlier references to the children of Israel who were also known as the Hebrews.

During the reign of Thutmose III, whose throne name was Men-kheper-Re, there is a reference in Egyptian records to the Hebrews. During his reign, a garrison of Egyptian soldiers attacked the city of **Joppa** along the Mediterranean coast in Canaan. The inscription reads: "Bring in the horses and give them feed lest an **Apir'** pass by [and steal] them. So they guarded the horses and gave them feed." (ANET 22)

Assuming that either Thutmose I or Thutmose II was the Exodus Pharaoh. If Thutmose III reigned for 54 years, as Egyptian records indicate, he would have been alive when Joshua and the Hebrews first entered the land of Canaan. So evidently on hearing these reports they seemed to be worried about an attack by the Hebrews on their property.

Interesting because Joshua 19:46 mentions that Israel took possession of the region near **Joppa** which was given to the tribe of Dan to settle in. The name **"Apiru" or "Apr"** is the Egyptian word phonetically equivalent to the word **"Hebrew."**

Another early mention of the Hebrews as well as their advance into the land of Canaan is found in letters known as the Amarna letters. These letters were written by Canaanite leaders requesting aid from the Egyptians in stopping the advancing Hebrew armies. One such letter also gives reference indirectly to the leader of the Hebrews, Joshua. It states:

"May the king, my lord, know that the **chief of the Apiru (Hebrew) has besieged the lands** which your god has given me; but I have attacked him. Also let the king, my lord, know that none of my allies have come to my aid, it is only I and Abdu-Heba who fight against the **'Apiru (Hebrew) chief**."

Amarna letter #RA xix p.106 (ANET 487)

Another fascinating inscription has been found which dates to the reign of Thutmose III. According to the Bible, Jacob was given a new name by God who said he would be called Israel (yisra'el) in Genesis 32:28. Yisra meaning "To prevail" and "El" meaning God. According to the Bible, Jacob and his sons entered into the land of Egypt when his son Joseph became second to Pharaoh. (Genesis 47:11) Their descendants lived there until the time of the Exodus. Amazingly there is an inscription from the time of Thutmose III at Karnak which lists cities and territories under his control. One name on the list is the territory referred to as "**Jacob-El**" and another is "**Joseph-EL.**" (ANET 242)

That is just totally Awesome!

Another tribal territory of the Hebrews mentioned in Egyptian records comes from the reign of Ramses III which mention the priestly tribe of Levi, inscribed with the words "**Levi-EL.**"

There is even more evidence. For example, we know that the Hebrews were divided into tribes and that one of their main means of livelihood was raising sheep. Today we would call them bedouin shepherds. The Egyptians had a name for them which was "Shasu" (those who traveled on foot). This was a generic term for tribes from many different places. But sometimes they got specific. For example, there is an Egyptian inscription from the time of Amenhotep III which mentions the "**Shasu of Yhw (Yahweh).**" (The foot tribes that followed Yahweh, the God of the Bible.) This is likely a reference to those Israelites who did not reside in a specific city, but lived in the countryside tending their sheep.

Inscription reads:
"Shasu of Yhw"
Yahweh = Jehovah

Other inscriptions back up this connection of the Hebrews with specific Shasu tribes. For example there is a reference from a military campaign of the Egyptian Pharaoh Seti I which identifies the Apiru (Hebrews) and Shasu as being the same.

They are known as the Beth-Shan steles, both of which account the same military campaign of Seti I into the land of Israel during the first year of his reign.

The first stela states: **"the foe belonging to the Shasu** are plotting rebellion. Their tribal chiefs are gathered in one place, waiting on the **mountain ranges of Kharu** (Israel/Syria)." ANET 254(a)

Another inscription reads: "The desolation which the mighty arm of Pharaoh . . . made among the **foe belonging to Shasu** from the fortress of Sile to the **Canaan**." ANET 254(c)

The second BethShan Stela of Seti I, which records the same military campaign, states:

"The **Apiru** of Mount **Yarmuta** with Teyer have risen in attack upon the people of **Rehem** . . . His majesty commanded a certain number of soldiers from his infantry and his numerous chariots to turn their attention to the foreign country of **Djahi**."

(ANET 255)

Djahi is the watershed country stretching from the Dead Sea north along the Lower Jordan to the sea of Galilee and then north along the upper Jordan river stretching as far north to the Orontes river, this was in the hands of Israel during their conquest of Canaan.

Yarmuta is the Biblical city of **Jarmuth**, and the region around it was in fact under the control of the Israelites according to Joshua 21:29. So this proves the Apiru were definitely one of the names the Egyptians used to refer to the Hebrews.

And since there is only one mountain range mentioned in the BethShan steles and that is Mount Yarmuta of the Apiru. The Apiru and Shasu in these inscriptions can be pretty well assumed as being the same enemy the Egyptians said they were fighting against.

Another Egyptian inscription from Pharaoh Amenhotep II also makes a connection between the Apiru and Shasu. At the end of his second Asiatic campaign, Amenhotep II erected a stele at Memphis on which he gave a list of booty he had collected, on which he lists the Apiru and Shasu side by side. It states:

"List of the plunder which his majesty carried off: Princes of Retenu (Syria): 127, Brothers of princes: 179, **Apiru: 3,600, Shasu (Bedouin): 15,200.**" (ANET 247)

GOD'S GREATEST WORDS TO ISRAEL

"And it shall come to pass, That whoever calls on the name of the Lord shall be saved.

"Men of Israel, hear these words: Jesus of Nazareth, a Man attested by God to you by miracles, wonders, and signs which God did through Him in your midst, as you yourselves also know; "Him, being delivered by the determined purpose and foreknowledge of God, you have taken by lawless hands, have crucified, and put to death; "whom God raised up, having loosed the pains of death, because it was not possible that He should be held by it. "For David says concerning Him:

'I foresaw the LORD always before my face, For He is at my right hand, that I may not be shaken. Therefore my heart rejoiced, and my tongue was glad; Moreover my flesh also will rest in hope. For You will not leave my soul in Hades, Nor will You allow Your Holy One to see corruption. You have made known to me the ways of life; You will make me full of joy in Your presence.'

"Men and brethren, let me speak freely to you of the patriarch David, that he is both dead and buried, and his tomb is with us to this day. "Therefore, being a prophet, and knowing that God had sworn with an oath to him that of the fruit of his body, according to the flesh, He would raise up the Christ to sit on his throne, "he, foreseeing this, spoke concerning the resurrection of the Christ, that His soul was not left in Hades, nor did His flesh see corruption. "This Jesus God has raised up, of which we are all witnesses. "Therefore being exalted to the right hand of God, and having received from the Father the promise of the Holy Spirit, He poured out this which you now see and hear. "For David did not ascend into the heavens, but he says himself:

'The LORD said to my Lord, "Sit at My right hand, Till I make Your enemies Your footstool." '

"Therefore let all the house of Israel know assuredly that God has made this Jesus, whom you crucified, both Lord and Christ." Now when they heard this, they were cut to the heart, and said to Peter and the rest of the apostles, "Men and brethren, what shall we do?"

Then Peter said to them, "Repent, and let every one of you be baptized in the name of Jesus Christ for the remission of sins; and you shall receive the gift of the Holy Spirit." Acts 2:21-38

JOASH KING OF SAMARIA

During the chaos which ensued in Baghdad during America's war with Iraq, the national museum was ransacked by vandals and many valuable artifacts were stolen. One of the items that was stolen was an artifact from the Assyrian king Adad-Nirari III listing his victories over the surrounding countries. The artifact known as the Tell el Rimah Stela has an important Biblical significance because it mentions Joash, the king of Samaria. The artifact states the following:

"**Adad-nirari** . . . king of Assyria . . . I gathered my chariots and army and gave them orders to march to the land of Hatti. In just one year, I subdued the entire county of the Amurru as well as Hatti. I imposed upon them tax and tribute forever. I received the tribute of 2,000 talents of silver, 1,000 talents of copper, 2,000 talents of iron, and 3,000 garments with multicolored trim from Mari of the land of Damascus. I also **received the tribute of Joash, the Samarian**, as well as the rulers of Tyre and of Sidon."

Tell el Rimah Stela
Mentions Joash
king of Samaria

Another separate Assyrian artifact, from the same Assyrian king, known as the Calah Orthostat Slab, also gives a similar account. It says:

"I subdued from the bank of the Euphrates, the whole land of Hatti, Amurru, Tyre, Sidon, the land of **Omri (Israel)**, Edom, and the land of Philistia, as far as the great sea in the west. I imposed taxes and tribute upon them.

I also marched to the land of Damascus. I confined **Mari, the king of Damascus** to the city of Damascus, his royal city."

These artifacts also make reference to Mari of Damascus which is most likely a reference to the Syrian king Hazael. On the inscription mentioning Joash, Mari may also possibly refer to Hazael's son Ben-Hadad, the Syrian ruler whom, in the Biblical account, Joash defeated in battle three times.

Another artifact found in northern Syria, and dated to the reign of Joash, also mentions Ben Hadad. The find known as the Zakir Stela states:

"I am Zakir, king of Hamath . . . **Benhadad, the son of Hazael, king of Aram**, united a group of ten kings against me." ANET 655

The Biblical account of Joash begins in 2King 13:14 where he has an encounter with the prophet Elisha:

"Elisha had become sick with the illness of which he would die. Then Joash the king of Israel came down to him, and wept over his face, and said, "O my father, my father, the chariots of Israel and their horsemen!"

And Elisha said to him, "Take a bow and some arrows." So he took himself a bow and some arrows. Then he said to the king of Israel, "Put your hand on the bow."

So he put his hand on it, and Elisha put his hands on the king's hands.

And he said, "Open the east window"; and he opened it. Then Elisha said, "Shoot"; and he shot.

And he said, "The arrow of the Lord's deliverance and the arrow of deliverance from Syria; for you must strike the Syrians at Aphek till you have destroyed them."

Then he said, "Take the arrows"; so he took them. And he said to the king of Israel, "Strike the ground"; so he struck three times, and stopped. And the man of God was angry with him, and said, "You should have struck five or six times; then you would have struck Syria till you had destroyed it! But now you will strike Syria only three times."

. . . And Hazael king of Syria oppressed Israel all the days of Jehoahaz. But the LORD was gracious to them, had compassion on them, and regarded them, because of His covenant with Abraham, Isaac, and Jacob, and would not yet destroy them or cast them from His presence. Now Hazael king of Syria died. Then Ben-Hadad his son reigned in his place.

And Jehoash the son of Jehoahaz recaptured from the hand of Ben-Hadad, the son of Hazael, the cities which he had taken out of the hand of Jehoahaz his father by war. Three times Joash defeated him and recaptured the cities of Israel.
2 Kings 13:14-25

JUST LIKE ISRAEL WHO SINNED, THE LORD REBUKES THOSE WHOM HE LOVES.

"You should know in your heart that as a man chastens his son, so the LORD your God chastens you. Deuteronomy 8:5

For whom the LORD loves He chastens, And scourges every son whom He receives."
Hebrews 12:6

AND THEN HE HAS COMPASSION UPON US.

"The LORD is gracious and full of compassion, Slow to anger and great in mercy. The LORD is good to all, And His tender mercies are over all His works."
Psalms 145:8-9

"For He remembered that they were but flesh, A breath that passes away and does not come again. How often they provoked Him in the wilderness, And grieved Him in the desert!
Yes, again and again they tempted God, And limited the Holy One of Israel. They did not remember His power: The day when He redeemed them from the enemy." Psalms 78:39-42:

Remember, Jesus Christ redeemed you from the penalty of sin and from our enemy Satan.

MENAHEM

Located within the Israel Museum is an artifact known as the Iran Stele, named after the place where it was discovered. The artifact records the military campaigns of the Assyrian ruler Tiglath-Pileser during his first nine years as king.

Iran Stele mentions
Menahem of Samaria

The text on this artifact also mentions that King Menahem of Israel, who reigned in Samaria, sent him a gift of silver, and that because of this gift he allowed Menahem to continue to rule.

The text states: "I received tribute from . . . Rezon of Damascus, Menahem of Samaria, Hiram of Tyre, . . . gold, silver, . . ." ANET 283

"In my former campaigns I considered all the cities . . . that I carried away as booty and . . . only in Samaria did I leave their king." ANET 283

This matches the Biblical account in 2Kings 15:19-20:

"Pul (Tiglath-Pileser) king of Assyria came against the land; and Menahem gave Pul a thousand talents of silver, that his hand might be with him to strengthen the kingdom under his control. And Menahem exacted the money from Israel, from all the very wealthy, from each man fifty shekels of silver, to give to the king of Assyria. So the king of Assyria turned back, and did not stay there in the land."

Tiglath-Pileser Profile from the walls of his palace. British Museum

Menahem was a brutal man who showed little compassion for his fellow man. He was so brutal that during one of his attacks upon a city in his own country that he had all the women, who were with child, ripped open so that he would guarantee all the infants of the city would be slain.

The first century Jewish historian Josephus wrote in his work Antiquities of the Jews concerning Menahem: "Now when Zachariah, the son of Jeroboam, had reigned six months over Israel, he was slain by the treachery of a certain friend of his, whose name was Shallum, the son of Jabesh, who took the kingdom afterward, but kept it no longer than thirty days; for Menahem, the general of his army, who was at that time in the city Tirzah, and heard of what had befallen Zachariah, removed thereupon with all his forces to Samaria, and joining battle with Shallum, slew him; and when he had made himself king, he went thence, and came to the city Tiphsah; but the citizens that were in it shut their gates, and barred them against the king, and would not admit him: but in order to be avenged on them, he burnt the country round about it, and took the city by force, upon a siege; and being very much displeased at what the inhabitants of Tiphsah had done, he slew them all, and spared not so much as the infants, without omitting the utmost instances of cruelty and barbarity; for he used such severity upon his own countrymen, as would not be pardonable with regard to strangers who had been conquered by him. And after this manner it was that this Menahem continued to reign with cruelty and barbarity for ten years. But when Pul, king of Assyria, had made an expedition against him, he did not wish to fight or engage in battle with the Assyrians, but he persuaded him to accept a thousand talents of silver, and to go away, and so put an end to the war. This sum the multitude collected for Menahem, by exacting fifty drachme as poll-money from every person. Afterwards he died, and was buried in Samaria, and he left his son Pekahiah, his successor, in charge of the kingdom, who followed the barbarity of his father."

Antiquities of the Jews, Book 9 section 228

MENAHEM WAS A CRUEL SHEPHERD
JESUS IS THE GOOD SHEPHERD

"Son of man, prophesy against the shepherds of Israel, prophesy and say to them, 'Thus says the Lord GOD to the shepherds: "Woe to the shepherds of Israel who feed themselves! Should not the shepherds feed the flocks? "You eat the fat and clothe yourselves with the wool; you slaughter the fatlings, but you do not feed the flock. "The weak you have not strengthened, nor have you healed those who were sick, nor bound up the broken, nor brought back what was driven away, nor sought what was lost; but with force and cruelty you have ruled them.

"So they were scattered because there was no shepherd; and they became food for all the beasts of the field when they were scattered. "My sheep wandered through all the mountains, and on every high hill; yes, My flock was scattered over the whole face of the earth, and no one was seeking or searching for them."

'Therefore, you shepherds, hear the word of the LORD: "as I live," says the Lord GOD, "surely because My flock became a prey, and My flock became food for every beast of the field, because there was no shepherd, nor did My shepherds search for My flock, but the shepherds fed themselves and did not feed My flock"; 'therefore, O shepherds, hear the word of the LORD! 'Thus says the Lord GOD: "Behold, I am against the shepherds, and I will require My flock at their hand; I will cause them to cease feeding the sheep, and the shepherds shall feed themselves no more; for I will deliver My flock from their mouths, that they may no longer be food for them."

'For thus says the Lord GOD: "Indeed I Myself will search for My sheep and seek them out. "As a shepherd seeks out his flock on the day he is among his scattered sheep, so will I seek out My sheep and deliver them from all the places where they were scattered on a cloudy and dark day. "And I will bring them out from the peoples and gather them from the countries, and will bring them to their own land; I will feed them on the mountains of Israel, in the valleys and in all the inhabited places of the country. "I will feed them in good pasture, and their fold shall be on the high mountains of Israel. There they shall lie down in a good fold and feed in rich pasture on the mountains of Israel. "I will feed My flock, and I will make them lie down," says the Lord GOD. "I will seek what was lost and bring back what was driven away, bind up the broken and strengthen what was sick; but I will destroy the fat and the strong, and feed them in judgment."

'And as for you, O My flock, thus says the Lord GOD: "Behold, I shall judge between sheep and sheep, between rams and goats. "Is it too little for you to have eaten up the good pasture, that you must tread down with your feet the residue of your pasture; and to have drunk of the clear waters, that you must foul the residue with your feet? "And as for My flock, they eat what you have trampled with your feet, and they drink what you have fouled with your feet."

'Therefore thus says the Lord GOD to them: "Behold, I Myself will judge between the fat and the lean sheep. "Because you have pushed with side and shoulder, butted all the weak ones with your horns, and scattered them abroad, "therefore I will save My flock, and they shall no longer be a prey; and I will judge between sheep and sheep. "I will establish one shepherd over them, and he shall feed them; My servant David. He shall feed them and be their shepherd. "And I, the LORD, will be their God, and My servant David a prince among them; I, the LORD, have spoken. Ezekiel 34:2-24

THE OFFSPRING OF DAVID IS THE GOOD SHEPHERD

"I, Jesus, have sent My angel to testify to you these things in the churches. I am the Root and the Offspring of David, the Bright and Morning Star."
Revelation 22:16

THE GREATEST WORDS FROM THE MOUTH OF THE GOOD SHEPHERD

"I am the good shepherd. The good shepherd gives His life for the sheep. "But a hireling, he who is not the shepherd, one who does not own the sheep, sees the wolf coming and leaves the sheep and flees; and the wolf catches the sheep and scatters them. "The hireling flees because he is a hireling and does not care about the sheep.

"I am the good shepherd; and I know My sheep, and am known by My own. "As the Father knows Me, even so I know the Father; and I lay down My life for the sheep. "Therefore My Father loves Me, because I lay down My life that I may take it again. "No one takes it from Me, but I lay it down of Myself. I have power to lay it down, and I have power to take it again. This command I have received from My Father." John 10:11-18

TIRHAKAH KING OF ETHIOPIA

In one of the first battles for Jerusalem, where God intervenes and destroys the army of Assyria, the Lord causes a rumor to be circulated amongst the Assyrians that the powerful king Tirhakah, who ruled over Ethiopia, was advancing toward Assyria.

The history surrounding Tirhakah is well documented in the annals of archaeology. Tirhakah is mentioned two times in the Bible.

In 2 Kings chapter 19, as well as the parallel account in Isaiah chapter 37, the Assyrian king Sennacherib comes down on a military campaign against Israel and surrounds King Hezekiah at Jerusalem.

The account begins in 2 Kings 19:8: "Then the **Rabshakeh** returned and found the king of Assyria warring against Libnah, for he heard that he had departed from **Lachish**.

And the king heard concerning **Tirhakah king of Ethiopia**, "Look, he has come out to make war with you."

So he again sent messengers to Hezekiah, saying, "Thus you shall speak to Hezekiah king of Judah, saying: "Do not let your God in whom you trust deceive you, saying, Jerusalem shall not be given into the hand of the king of Assyria."

'Look! You have heard what the kings of Assyria have done to all lands by utterly destroying them; and shall you be delivered?

'Have the gods of the nations delivered those whom my fathers have destroyed, Gozan and Haran and Rezeph, and the people of Eden who were in Telassar?

'**Where is the king of Hamath**, **the king of Arpad**, and the king of the city of **Sepharvaim . . ?**

These statements by the Assyrians have been confirmed in archaeology. For example Sennacherib's victory at Lachish mentioned in 2Kings 19:8 has been confirmed on Assyrian artifacts. On a wall from the palace of Sennacherib the following inscription mentions his victory at Lachish:

"Sennacherib, the king over all, king of Assyria, sat upon a throne and viewed the plunder taken from **Lachish.**" (ANET 288)

Siege of Lachish - Sennacherib's Palace Wall

Another confirmation is mentioned in 2Kings 18:17-18: "Then the king of Assyria sent the **Tartan, the Rabsaris, and the Rabshakeh from Lachish**, with a great army against Jerusalem, to King Hezekiah."

All three of these Assyrian titles have been found in archaeology. Dating back to the reign of Shalmaneser III, a fragment of an ancient tablet mentions the titles of certain Assyrian high officials. It mentions **"Turtanu (Tartan) and Rabsaqe (Rabshakeh)."** Another artifact, a clay tablet dated to 645 B.C., makes mention of the title **Rabsaris**. It is inscribed with the words: **"Limmu of Rabsaris Nabusarusur."**

Then in 2Kings 19:13 the Assyrians remind Hezekiah of past victories attained by previous Assyrian rulers over Judah and the kings surrounding their country. Three of them mentioned are the kings of **Hamath, Arpad and Sepharvaim**.

An artifact known as the Nimrud inscription by Sargon II, who was the father of Sennacherib, mentions Hamath as follows: "Sargon, the **master over the land of Judah** which is far away, the **conqueror of Hamath**." (ANET 287)

So this victory over Judah and Hamath would have been fresh in the minds of Hezekiah and the residents of Jerusalem.

Two artifacts known as the Tel Sheik Hammad Stela and the Orthostat Slab, from Adadnirari III, mention the conquest of **Arpad**. The latter states:

"Atarshumki (Arpad's king) . . . came forward to battle. I defeated him and his army. I took treasure from his palace and carried it off."

Many years earlier another Assyrian king, Tiglath-Pileser II, laid siege to Arpad and massacred its citizens and utterly destroyed the city. It took Tiglath-Pileser three years to take Arpad because it was a fortress city with a two mile long defense wall that was up to 25 foot high. It was thought at that time to be an impenetrable fortress. So what the Assyrians were basically telling Hezekiah was that if he thought he was safe within the city walls of Jerusalem, then he better think again.

Another city mentioned in 2Kings 19:13 was the city of **Sepharvaim**, whose name refers to a two-part city. Many believe this was the city of **Sippar** on the east side of the Euphrates river, while its sister city, **Akkad**, was on the west. These cities were indeed conquered by Sennacherib as mentioned on the following artifact:

"In the third year of Belibni; Sennacherib marched against the country of Akkad and carried

away the goods plundered from **Akkad** . . . Sennacherib then placed his son Ashurnadinshumi upon the throne there (at the city of Akkad) . . . Afterwards, the king of Elam counterattacked the Akkadians . . . entered **Sippar and killed its inhabitants** . . . **and captured Ashurnadinshumi** and brought him to Elam . . . Later Sennacherib marched against Elam and demolished the country."
(ANET 301-302)

So these artifacts definitely confirm the history behind the Assyrians threats being made to Hezekiah. To see more artifacts mentioning Sennacherib's encampment against King Hezekiah, see Chapter 23 of our first volume, Bible Believer's Archaeology - Historical Evidence that Proves the Bible.

Now as to Tirhakah, who ruled over Ethiopia, mentioned in 2Kings 19:9, his story is a very interesting one indeed. He is mentioned multiple times by King Esarhaddon who was the son of Sennacherib. From the British Museum there is an artifact from Esarhaddon that reads:

"During my military actions I threw up earthworks for a siege against Ba'lu, the king of Tyre, who had put his faith in his friend **Tirhakah king of Nubia** to defend him . . . I marched directly toward Meluhha, a distance of 30 double hours from the town of Apku which is in the land of **Samaria**."
(ANET 292)

From Tyre, Esarhaddon then marches against Egypt and Ethiopia as mentioned on the following two artifacts:

"I conquered the island of Tyre in the sea. I plundered all the towns and the possessions of king Ba'lu, who had befriended **Tirhakah the king of Nubia**. I conquered Egypt, Paturisi, and Nubia. It's king, **Tirhakah**, I shot five times with arrows and took control over his entire land. Many kings from amidst the sea, from the country of Cyprus, as far as Tarisi, bowed down to my feet and from them I received honor." (ANET 290)

The second artifact from Esarhaddon, known as the Senjirli Stela states: "From the town of Ishupri all the way to Memphis, his royal residence, a distance of 15 days march, I fought daily, without ceasing, a very bloody war with **Tirhakah, the king of Egypt and Ethiopia,** the one whom I hate . . . Five times I hit him with the point of my arrows, wounding him, . . . and then I laid siege to Memphis, his royal palace, and conquered it in half a day." (ANET 293)

Senjirli Stela of Esarhaddon

After Esarhaddon dies, his son Ashurbanipal ascends to the throne. When Tirhakah once again begins to cause trouble for the Assyrians, Ashurbanipal leads his armies against Egypt and Ethiopia, just like his father had done previously.

An artifact located in the British Museum known as the Rassam Cylinder of Ashurbanipal details these events:

"In my first expedition I marched against **Tirhakah king of Egypt and Nubia**, whom Esarhaddon, king of Assyria, my own father, had defeated and in whose land he was king. This same Tirhakah gave little thought to the power of Ashur. . . . He rebelled against the kings and his regents whom my own father had appointed to rule over Egypt. He took control and set up his residence at Memphis, the city which my own father had conquered and made subject to the Assyrian empire. A courier was dispatched to me at Nineveh with an urgent report of these things. I became furious on account of these reports . . . So I called to arms my great army . . . and they advanced by the shortest possible route to Egypt and Ethiopia. During my march to Egypt, 22 kings from along the sea, Islands and the mainland, those who were my subjects, brought great tribute to me and kissed my feet. I made these kings accompany my army as I passed through their lands." (A list of these various kings are listed on Esarhaddon's Prism - ANET 291, they included "**Manasseh king of Judah**.")

"I advanced rapidly . . . to bring relief to the kings and governors of Egypt, those servants who are loyal to me. Tirhakah the king of Egypt and Nubia heard in Memphis that his army was defeated by the overwhelming majesty of Ashur and he became like a madman . . . he left Memphis, in order to save his life, and fled to Thebes. I then led my army against this town and seized it as well.

Necho, king of Memphis, . . . As well as Mantimanhe, king of Thebes, these kings, governors and officials who were left in charge by my father in Egypt, who had fled their positions during the rebellion of Tirhakah and had scattered throughout the land, I reinstated them to their former posts (as rulers in Egypt) . . .

Afterwards, these same rulers whom I had reinstated broke their allegiance to me, and did not keep their agreements . . . , they forgot that I had treated them with mercy and they hatched a plan of conspiracy. They talked about rebellion and came to a conclusion, saying to themselves: "Tirhakah has been driven out of Egypt, how can we ourselves hope to stay here?" . . . And they sent messengers to Tirhakah, the king of Nubia, to establish an alliance saying: "Let peace reign between us and let us come to a mutual agreement to divide the land amongst ourselves in order that no foreigner shall rule over us!" . . .

My officers heard about these rumors and intercepted their messengers carrying their proposals bound for Tirhakah and so the plot of their rebellion was uncovered. They arrested these kings and put their hands and feet into iron cuffs with chains.

. . . Those kings who had repeatedly schemed against me were brought alive to me at Nineveh. From all of them, I had mercy only upon Necho and spared his life. I made a treaty with him that he pledged to honor which greatly surpassed those of the former treaty." (ANET 294-295)

Rassam Cylinder
Of Ashurbanapal
British Museum

This alliance between Necho and Assyria would later be reinforced when his son Necho II would lead an expedition to Assyria and come to the aid of an Assyrian ruler fighting against the invading armies of Babylon. At this time, Necho II would then be hampered on his journey by King Josiah of Judah, whom Necho's armies would defeat as recorded in 2Kings 23:29.

So as you can see, both the Ethiopian king Tirhakah, and the Necho dynasty in Egypt, are confirmed in the pages of ancient history as important players in the Biblical accounts.

These battles fought by the Assyrians against king Tirhakah also fulfilled the prophet Isaiah's words which he had spoken against Egypt and Ethiopia as prophesied in Isaiah 20:1-6:

"In the year that Tartan came to Ashdod, when Sargon the king of Assyria sent him, and he fought against Ashdod and took it, at the same time the LORD spoke by Isaiah the son of Amoz, saying, "Go, and remove the sackcloth from your body, and take your sandals off your feet." And he did so, walking naked and barefoot.

Then the LORD said, "Just as My servant Isaiah has walked naked and barefoot three years for a sign and a wonder against Egypt and Ethiopia, "so shall the king of Assyria lead away the Egyptians as prisoners and the Ethiopians as captives, young and old, naked and barefoot, with their buttocks uncovered, to the shame of Egypt.

"Then they shall be afraid and ashamed of Ethiopia their expectation and Egypt their glory. "And the inhabitant of this territory will say in that day, 'Surely such is our expectation, wherever we flee for help to be delivered from the king of Assyria; and how shall we escape?'"

WHO WILL LISTEN TO THE LORD AND CONFESS THEIR SINS BEFORE HIM?

"Who among you will give ear to this? Who will listen and hear for the time to come? Who gave Jacob for plunder, and Israel to the robbers? Was it not the LORD, He against whom we have sinned? For they would not walk in His ways, Nor were they obedient to His law. Therefore He has poured on him the fury of His anger And the strength of battle; It has set him on fire all around, Yet he did not know; And it burned him, Yet he did not take it to heart.

But now, thus says the LORD, who created you, O Jacob, And He who formed you, O Israel:

"Fear not, for I have redeemed you; I have called you by your name; You are Mine. When you pass through the waters, I will be with you; And through the rivers, they shall not overflow you. When you walk through the fire, you shall not be burned, Nor shall the flame scorch you. For I am the LORD your God, The Holy One of Israel, your Savior; I gave Egypt for your ransom, Ethiopia and Seba in your place.

Since you were precious in My sight, You have been honored, And I have loved you; Therefore I will give men for you, And people for your life . . . Bring My sons from afar, And My daughters from the ends of the earth; Everyone who is called by My name, Whom I have created for My glory; I have formed him, yes, I have made him." Bring out the blind people who have eyes, And the deaf who have ears.

Let all the nations be gathered together, And let the people be assembled. Who among them can declare this, And show us former things? Let them bring out their witnesses, that they may be justified; Or let them hear and say, "It is truth."

"You are My witnesses," says the LORD, "And My servant whom I have chosen, That you may know and believe Me, And understand that I am He. Before Me there was no God formed, Nor shall there be after Me. I, even I, am the LORD, And besides Me there is no savior.

I have declared and saved, I have proclaimed, And there was no foreign god among you; Therefore you are My witnesses," Says the LORD, "that I am God. Indeed before the day was, I am He; And there is no one who can deliver out of My hand; I work, and who will reverse it?" Thus says the LORD, your Redeemer, The Holy One . . . you have burdened Me with your sins, You have wearied Me with your iniquities. "I, even I, am He who blots out your transgressions for My own sake; And I will not remember your sins.

Put Me in remembrance; Let us contend together; State your case, that you may be acquitted." Isaiah 42:23-43:26

JOSIAH'S BATTLE WITH NECHO

The events that surround the last days of King Josiah are chronicled in the pages of ancient history.

The first major event that takes place during the last few years of his reign is the fall of the Assyrian capital of Nineveh.

The prophecy against Nineveh and the fall of the Assyrian empire is given in Zephaniah 2:13: "And He (God) will stretch out his hand against the north, to Destroy Assyria, and make Nineveh a desolation, as dry as the wilderness."

The fall of Nineveh and the Assyrian Empire is indeed mentioned in an artifact known as the Babylonian Chronicles located within the British Museum. It describes the following events which occurred around 612 B.C.:

"In the fourteenth year of Nabopolassar, the king of Akkad called up his army. Cyaxares, the king of the Manda-hordes (the Medes), also marched out to meet the king of Akkad . . . and they joined forces . . . They marched on the banks of the Tigris river and . . . encamped against Nineveh . . . Three battles were fought, then they made a great attack against the city . . . On that day Sinsharishkun, king of Assyria was defeated . . . and the city was turned into a pile of rubble . . . but the army of Assyria escaped . . . Ashuruballit . . . became the new king of Assyria and reigned in Harran." ANET 304-305

So Zephaniah's prophecy against Nineveh became fulfilled.

The next event leading to Assyria's complete downfall occurs two years later when the Akkadian king attacks the new Assyrian capital at Harran. The Babylonian Chronicle continues:

"The Manda-hordes . . . came to the aid of the king of Akkad and they merged their armies and marched against Harran, against Ashuruballit. Fear of the enemy befell Ashuruballit and his soldiers . . . and they left the town. The King of Akkad arrived at Harran and seized the city." (BM21901, ANET 305)

At this time, Assyria sends a dispatch to Egypt requesting help from the Egyptian king Necho II, whose father had formed a treaty years earlier with the Assyrians. Necho II then takes his army and heads north to aid the Assyrians. But on his way, Josiah the king of Judah brings out his army to intercept the Egyptians at Megiddo. This battle is recorded in 2 Chronicles 35:20:

"After all this, when Josiah had prepared the temple, Necho king of Egypt came up to fight against Carchemish by the Euphrates; and Josiah went out against him. But he sent messengers to him, saying, "What have I to do with you, king of Judah? I have not come against you this day, but against the house with which I have war; for God commanded me to make haste. Refrain from meddling with God, who is with me, lest He destroy you."

Nevertheless Josiah would not turn his face from him, but disguised himself so that he might fight with him, and did not heed the words of Necho from the mouth of God. So he came to fight in the Valley of Megiddo. And the archers shot King Josiah; and the king said to his servants, "Take me away, for I am severely wounded."

His servants therefore took him out of that chariot and put him in the second chariot that he had, and they brought him to Jerusalem. So he died, and was buried in one of the tombs of his fathers. And all Judah and Jerusalem mourned for Josiah."

The main core of the Egyptian army then advances northward to help the Assyrians who had assembled at Carchemish awaiting Necho's army in order to attack the Babylonians at Harran.

This event occurs during the same year as Josiah's death in 609 B.C. and is verified in the Babylonian Chronicles as follows;

"Seventeenth year of Nabopolassar, Ashur-uballit II king of Assyria and a large army of Egypt (that of Necho II who had come to his aid) crossed the river Euphrates and marched on to conquer Harran. His army entered it, but the garrison which the king of Akkad (Nabopolassar) had left there defeated them and so he encamped against Harran. He continued to make attacks against the town. However nothing was accomplished and they returned (to Carchemish)." (BM21901, ANET 305)

At the same time, a contingent of the Egyptian army advances back towards Jerusalem and captures Jehoahaz, who reigned only three months over Judah, and Necho sends him to Egypt as a prisoner in chains. Necho then installs Jehoiakim as ruler in Jerusalem. This is recorded in 2 Chronicles chapter 36.

Four years after these events, in 605 B.C., another Biblical prophecy comes to pass, the destruction of the city of Carchemish and the Egyptian army located near the Euphrates river. This is stated in Jeremiah 46:1-10:

"The word of the LORD which came to Jeremiah the prophet against the nations. Against Egypt. Concerning the army of **Pharaoh Necho, king of Egypt, which was by the River Euphrates in Carchemish, and which Nebuchadnezzar king of Babylon defeated in the fourth year of Jehoiakim** the son of Josiah, king of Judah: "Order the buckler and shield, And draw near to battle! Harness the horses, And mount up, you horsemen! Stand forth with your helmets, Polish the spears, Put on the armor! Why have I seen them dismayed and turned back? **Their mighty ones are beaten down; They have speedily fled,** And did not look back, For fear was all around," says the LORD. **"Do not let the swift flee away, Nor the mighty man escape; They will stumble and fall Toward the north, by the River Euphrates.** "Who is this coming up like a flood, Whose waters move like the rivers? Egypt rises up like a flood, And its waters move like the rivers; And he says, 'I will go up and cover the earth, I will destroy the city and its inhabitants.' Come up, O horses, and rage, O chariots! And let the mighty men come forth: The Ethiopians and the Libyans who handle the shield, And the Lydians who handle and bend the bow. For this is the day of the Lord GOD of hosts, A day of vengeance, That He may avenge Himself on His adversaries. The sword shall devour; It shall be satiated and made drunk with their blood; **For the Lord GOD of hosts has a sacrifice In the north country by the River Euphrates."**

This battle between the Egyptian army under Necho's command and the Babylonian forces led by

Nebuchadnezzar is recorded almost blow by blow in the Babylonian Chronicles. It states:

"In the twentieth year (of Nabopolassar, 606 B.C.) . . . The army of Egypt, which was at Carchemish, crossed the Euphrates, and against the army of Akkad, which was camped at Quramatu, it marched. They pushed back the army of Akkad so that they withdrew. (BM 22047)

"In the twenty first year (of Nabopolassar, 605 B.C.) . . . Nebuchadnezzar his eldest son, the crown prince, mustered the Babylonian army and took command of his troops, **he then marched to Carchemish, which is on the bank of the Euphrates, to go against the Egyptian army which lay at Carchemish.**

They fought with each other and the **Egyptian army withdrew before him . . . As for the rest of the Egyptian army, which had escaped from defeat so quickly that no weapons had reached them, the Babylonian troops overtook them in the district of Hamath and defeated them so that not a single man was able to escape to his own country.**" (BM 21946)

In the past God cutoff Egypt, Assyria and Israel. But in the Future, they will serve the Lord together:

Isaiah 19: "The burden against Egypt. Behold, the LORD rides on a swift cloud, And will come into Egypt; The idols of Egypt will totter at His presence, And the heart of Egypt will melt in its midst.

"I will set Egyptians against Egyptians; Everyone will fight against his brother, And everyone against his neighbor, City against city, kingdom against kingdom.

The spirit of Egypt will fail in its midst; I will destroy their counsel, And they will consult the idols and the charmers, The mediums and the sorcerers. And the Egyptians I will give Into the hand of a cruel master, And a fierce king will rule over them," Says the Lord, the LORD of hosts.

The waters will fail from the sea, And the river will be wasted and dried up. The rivers will turn foul; The brooks of defense will be emptied and dried up; The reeds and rushes will wither. The papyrus reeds by the River, by the mouth of the River, And everything sown by the River, Will wither, be driven away, and be no more. The fishermen also will mourn; All those will lament who cast hooks into the River, And they will languish who spread nets on the waters. Moreover those who work in fine flax and those who weave fine fabric will be ashamed; And its foundations will be broken. All who make wages will be troubled of soul.

Surely the princes of Zoan are fools; Pharaoh's wise counselors give foolish counsel. How do you say to Pharaoh, "I am the son of the wise, The son of ancient kings?" Where are they? Where are your wise men? Let them tell you now, And let them know what the LORD of hosts has purposed against Egypt. The princes of Zoan have become fools; The princes of Noph (the ancient city near present day Cairo) are deceived; They have also deluded Egypt, Those who are the mainstay of its tribes. The LORD has mingled a perverse spirit in her midst; And they have caused Egypt to err in all her work, As a drunken man staggers in his vomit. Neither will there be any work for Egypt, Which the head or tail, Palm branch or bulrush, may do.

In that day Egypt will be like women, and will be afraid and fear because of the waving of the hand of the LORD of hosts, which He waves over it. And the land of Judah will be a terror to Egypt; everyone who makes mention of it will be afraid in himself, because of the counsel of the LORD of hosts which He has determined against it. In that day five cities in the land of Egypt will speak the language of Canaan and swear by the LORD of hosts; one will be called the City of Destruction.

In that day there will be an altar to the LORD in the midst of the land of Egypt, and a pillar to the LORD at its border. And it will be for a sign and for a witness to the LORD of hosts in the land of Egypt; for they will cry to the LORD because of the oppressors, and **He will send them a Savior and a Mighty One, and He will deliver them. Then the LORD will be known to Egypt, and the Egyptians will know the LORD in that day**, and will make sacrifice and offering; yes, they will make a vow to the LORD and perform it.

And the LORD will strike Egypt, He will strike and heal it; they will return to the LORD, and He will be entreated by them and heal them.

In that day there will be a highway from Egypt to Assyria, and the Assyrian will come into Egypt and the Egyptian into Assyria, and the Egyptians will serve with the Assyrians. **In that day Israel will be one of three with Egypt and Assyria; a blessing in the midst of the land, whom the LORD of hosts shall bless, saying, "Blessed is Egypt My people, and Assyria the work of My hands, and Israel My inheritance."**

JEREMIAH - CHAPTER 39

In the month of July in the year of our Lord 2007, a cuneiform tablet which had been sitting dormant in the British Museum was deciphered and found to bear the name of a chief officer of Nebuchadnezzar, the king of Babylon. The name of this royal official was **Nebo-Sarsekim**, and he is mentioned in the Bible by Jeremiah the prophet in chapter 39 verse 3 of his Book.

The clay tablet is inscribed with the words:
"(In regards to the) 1.5 minas (24 ounces) of gold, the property of **Nabu-sharrussu-ukin, the chief eunuch**, which he sent via Arad-Banitu the eunuch to [the temple at] Esangila: Arad-Banitu delivered [it] to Esangila. In the presence of Bel-usat, the son of Alpaya, the royal bodyguard, [and of] Nadin, the son of Marduk-zer-ibni. Month XI, day 18, year 10 [in the reign of] Nebuchadnezzar, the king of Babylon."

Three other men that lived through Nebuchadnezzar's invasion of Jerusalem in 587 B.C., as described in Jeremiah 39, have also been previously confirmed in archaeology. The names of **Nebuzaradan** the captain of the guard mentioned in Jeremiah 39:9, along with **Nergal-Sharezer** who is listed alongside Nebo-Sarsekim in Jeremiah 39:3. The names were found on a clay prism from Babylon. The artifact also mentions the names of various officers in the court of Nebuchadnezzar. The translation of the prism is as follows:

" I gave orders to the following officials of my court to carry out their duties as royal officers: As high court officials **Nebuzeriddinam** (**Nebuzaradan**) . . . the officials of the land of Akkad (Babylon);

Eadaian, the governor of the lands along the Sea, **Nergalsharusur (Nergal-Sharezer)** the Sin-magir (who is listed along with other governors.)"

ANET 307-308

A separate artifact identified as belonging to **Gedaliah**, the same man who Nebuchadnezzar installed as governor over Judah, has also been discovered. He is mentioned in Jeremiah 39:14

Seal of Gedaliah

The Biblical account of when the lives of all these men came together is found in Jeremiah 39:

"In the ninth year of Zedekiah king of Judah, in the tenth month, Nebuchadnezzar king of Babylon and all his army came against Jerusalem, and besieged it. In the eleventh year of Zedekiah, in the fourth month, on the ninth day of the month, the city was penetrated. Then all the princes of the king of Babylon came in and sat in the Middle Gate: Nergal-Sharezer the Samgar, **Nebo-Sarsechim the Rabsaris** (rabsaris is a title meaning chief of the eunuchs), Nergal-Sarezer the Rabmag, with the rest of the princes of the king of Babylon. So it was, when Zedekiah the king of Judah and all the men of war saw them, that they fled and went out of the city by night, by way of the king's garden, by the gate between the two walls. And he went out by way of the plain.

But the Chaldean army pursued them and overtook Zedekiah in the plains of Jericho. And when they had captured him, they brought him up to Nebuchadnezzar king of Babylon, to Riblah in the land of Hamath, where he pronounced judgment on him. Then the king of Babylon killed the sons of Zedekiah before his eyes in Riblah; the king of Babylon also killed all the nobles of Judah. Moreover he put out Zedekiah's eyes, and bound him with bronze fetters to carry him off to Babylon.

And the Chaldeans burned the king's house and the houses of the people with fire, and broke down the walls of Jerusalem. Then **Nebuzaradan** the captain of the guard carried away captive to Babylon the remnant of the people who remained in the city and those who defected to him, with the rest of the people who remained. But Nebuzaradan the captain of the guard left in the land of Judah the poor people, who had nothing, and gave them vineyards and fields at the same time.

Now Nebuchadnezzar king of Babylon gave charge concerning Jeremiah to **Nebuzaradan** the captain of the guard, saying, "Take him and look after him, and do him no harm; but do to him just as he says to you." So Nebuzaradan the captain of the guard sent Nebushasban the Rabsaris, **Nergal-Sharezer the Rabmag**, and all the king of Babylon's chief officers; then they sent someone to take Jeremiah from the court of the prison, and committed him to **Gedaliah** the son of Ahikam, the son of Shaphan, that he should take him home. So he dwelt among the people.

Meanwhile the word of the LORD had come to Jeremiah while he was shut up in the court of the prison, saying, "Go and speak to Ebed-Melech the Ethiopian, saying, 'Thus says the LORD of hosts, the God of Israel: "Behold, I will bring My words upon this city for adversity and not for good, and they shall be performed in that day before you.

"But I will deliver you in that day," says the LORD, "and you shall not be given into the hand of the men of whom you are afraid. "For I will surely deliver you, and you shall not fall by the sword; but your life shall be as a prize to you, **because you have put your trust in Me," says the LORD.**'

TRUST IN THE LORD FOR YOUR DELIVERANCE:

"We had the sentence of death in ourselves, that **we should not trust in ourselves but in God** who raises the dead, **who delivered us** from so great a death, and does deliver us; in whom we trust that He will still deliver us." 2 Corinthians 1:9-10

"Grace to you and peace from God the Father and our **Lord Jesus Christ, who gave Himself for our sins, that He might deliver us** from this present evil age, according to the will of our God and Father, to whom be glory forever and ever. Amen."
Galatians 1:3-5

Old Testament   Chapter 16

DANIEL AND THE CIA AGENT

Like a page out of a James Bond movie, one of the great Biblical finds of archaeology is surrounded by adventure, mystery and intrigue.

Just a few years after World War II, the CIA had an agent operating in the Middle east by the name of Miles Copeland. In 1947 while he was on duty in Damascus, Copeland was secretly approached by a shady Egyptian merchant carrying a sackcloth in which he claimed was a great treasure hid inside. The merchant reached his dirt laden hands inside his cloth sack and pulled out an ancient scroll.

The scroll was so old that fragments from the parchment were flaking off onto the street below, the pieces being blown to and fro by the wind.

CIA agents were not exactly very secret back at this time since the merchant knew who Copeland was. Knowing Copeland's contacts with the American government, the Egyptian asked if he could help him identify the artifact. Copeland replied that he would help as long as the scroll was left with him to investigate it. The merchant agreed to his terms and left.

Copeland decided he would photograph the scroll and send the photos to an expert in ancient languages for identification. Since the scroll was very large he had to find a place where he could stretch out the scroll, so he decided upon the roof top located at the American Embassy. What he hadn't anticipated was the wind gusts that were blowing that day made this less than an ideal choice.

Wind or not, with the help of some of his colleagues, they began to unravel the scroll in order to get their photos. But this led to some very bad consequences. Fighting the wind, a large part of the deteriorating scroll flaked off into the sky, being blown off the rooftop like ashes from a fire.

Not knowing the importance of the scroll, little care was taken in the handling of this delicate scroll. Maybe had Copeland let his wife in on his little secret the artifact would have been handled with much more care, since Copeland's wife just happened to be an archaeologist.

None the less, Copeland was able to photograph the damaged scroll. He shot 30 frames of film to cover the entire length of the scroll. He then sent the photographs to the American Embassy in Beirut who passed them on to a man trained in ancient languages.

Upon analyzing the photos, the ancient writing expert found that part of the scroll was written in the ancient languages of Aramaic and Hebrew, and he identified the ancient artifact as the Biblical book of Daniel.

Upon hearing the news, Copeland set out in search for the merchant, but he was no where to be found. Whatever happened to the man is anybody's guess. And to make the story even more mysterious is the fact that someone from the CIA is believed to have confiscated the scroll along with the photographs and to this day no one knows where they are. History had lost a complete scroll of an ancient relic.

Fortunately during this same year in a place a little further away, a complete scroll of the book of Isaiah was uncovered, part of what we now know as the Dead Sea Scrolls

Copeland would find a little relief five years later when some fragments of the book of Daniel were found in one of the Dead Sea Scroll caves. Maybe just possibly some of those fragments were part of that same deteriorating scroll he once handled and photographed.

The fragments that were found in the Dead Sea scroll cave also verify the fact that the Book of Daniel was written during the time of Ancient Babylon.

You see for many years before these artifacts were found, liberal Bible critics claimed that the Book of Daniel could not have been written until the period between the first and second century B.C. because of the accuracy of Biblical prophecies Daniel had made concerning nations that would arise after Daniel's time. They claimed that scribes made up these stories much later on in history, because that was the only possible explanation, in their mind's, of how they could explain the knowledge of future kingdoms that Daniel predicted would arise. For example, Daniel living at the time of the Babylonians, predicted the rise of the Empire of Greece, gives a play by play account of how Alexander the Great's empire would later be divided amongst his four generals. Daniel predicts conflicts between the Ptolemies and the Seleucids over Israel, giving a historically accurate blow by blow play book. He also predicts the rise of Rome as a great empire, and predicted how a Syrian (Antiochus Epiphanes) would invade Jerusalem and desecrate the Temple around 164 B.C.

Daniel also predicts the date the Messiah, Jesus Christ, would be cut off (crucified), as well as the Romans destroying Jerusalem and the temple.

But because of the finding of the Daniel fragments these critics have been proven wrong. You ask why?

Well because of the language found on the Dead Sea Scroll fragments of Daniel.

You see if you open your Bible and look at Daniel 2:4, it says: "The Chaldeans spoke to the king in Aramaic" You see most of the Old Testament is written in Hebrew, But Daniel 2:46-7:28 is written in the Old Aramaic language. This is the language which was used at the time of the Babylonian empire. The fragments of the book of Daniel found along with the Dead Sea Scrolls retain the Old Aramaic sentence structure which goes subject, object, and verb in the sentences. But other Dead Sea Scroll writings written around 165 B.C. used a newer Aramaic language in which the word order goes subject, verb, and object. The linguistic characteristics of the Hebrew on the scroll has also since been dated to earlier than the second century before Christ, and the Aramaic is written in a way that strongly suggests it was originally penned. This proves that Daniel was written way before many of the prophecies about historical events that it predicted ever came to pass.

In Daniel's "seventy sevens" prophecy found in Daniel chapter 9, he predicts the very year Christ would be cutoff and die.

"Know therefore and understand, That from the going forth of the command to restore and rebuild Jerusalem (The command given in the twentieth year of Artaxerses (446 B.C.) as recorded in Nehemiah chapter 2) Until Messiah the Prince, there shall be seven sevens and sixty two sevens (A total of 69 seven year periods of time or 483 Biblical years.)

Note: Daniel used a 360 day prophetic year in his prophecies, not a 365 day year which we currently use today. This can be seen in Daniel 9:27 where he prophesied that the coming AntiChrist would make a end to sacrifice and offering in the middle of the seven year period of the tribulation, or three and a half years into it. So 360 days X 3.5 years = 1,260 days. This same prophecy is mentioned in Revelation 11:3 in which the two witnesses prophecy for 1,260 days before they are killed. Many of the Jews will then flee to the wilderness and be protected by God for another 1,260 days according to Revelation 12:6. Therefore the Scripture verifies that Daniel was using a 360 day calender year in his "seventy sevens" prophecy.

So getting back to the calculation as to when the Messiah would be cutoff. 483 Biblical calender years is equal to 476 years based on our current 365 day year. Therefore, 446 B.C. (20th year of Artaxerxes) - 476 years = 30 A.D., which is the year in which Daniel predicts Jesus would die. This amazingly matches the time frame referred to in the Gospels.

HOW TO BE RECONCILED TO GOD

Daniel states in Daniel 9:24 that Christ would come for one reason, "To make reconciliation for iniquity," just as Romans 5:8 says "God demonstrated His love towards us, in that while we were still sinners, Christ died for us. Much more now having been justified by His blood, we will be saved from wrath through Him. For if when we were enemies we were reconciled to God through the death of His Son, much more, having been reconciled, we shall be saved by His life."

ESTHER AND MORDECAI

In the very first passage of the book of Esther we are introduced to a controversial king by the name of Ahasuerus. Controversial because historians argue over which ruler this actually was.

You see the name Ahasuerus seems to have been used in the Bible for a couple of different kings.

The first one is mentioned in Daniel 9:1 where Ahasuerus is listed as the father of Darius the Mede. This Darius the Mede is believed to be the ruler the historian Xenophon records as Cyaxares II (also recorded as Gubaru or Gobyras). His father's name was Astyages. Therefore Astyages is one of the possible candidates for King Ahasuerus mentioned in Esther.

And if one interprets Esther 2:5-6 as meaning Mordecai was the one taken captive with Jehoiachin, as some believe, which happened in 597 B.C., then Astyages fits this king very well since Esther 1:3 states that the events happened in the third year of Ahasuerus. The third year in which Astyages ruled would have been around 583 B.C., just fourteen years after Mordecai's captivity.

In regards to his name, the Greek historian Ctesias around 400 B.C. calls Astyages 'Astuïgas', and the Babylonian rendering of his name is **Ištumegu**. 'Astyages' means 'sacker of cities' in Greek.

And since **Ištu** sounds very similar to Esther, it may be possible that one of Astyages' queens would have been known as Queen **Ištu**.

A reference to a son of a man named Marduka is also mentioned on an artifact found in Babylonian records which dates to the first year of Cyrus, and the first year of Darius the Mede who was governing in Babylon right after its fall.

This Marduka's name is similar in pronunciation to Mordecai. The artifact reads:

" . . . In the ascension year of Cyrus . . . Nergalsumibni son of Marduka (Mordecai?) . . . this tablet was written in the presence of Baurese the judge . . . Gobyras, Governor of Babylon . . ."

But there are a couple of problems with identifying Astyages as being the king and this Marduka as being Mordecai as mentioned in Esther.

First of all, it is stated in verse 1 of Esther that the empire of Ahasuerus stretched from India to Ethiopia, something the empire of Astyages was not known to encompass. The empire it seems wasn't expanded into Ethiopia until the time of Cambyses around 525 B.C.

Secondly, if one interprets Esther 2:6 as saying it was Mordecai's great-grandfather Kish, and not Mordecai, who was taken captive by Nebuchadnezzar along with King Jehoiachin in 597 B.C., it would be highly unlikely that Mordecai would have been alive at the time of Astyages.

The other king who some historians believe to be the Ahasuerus of the book of Esther is the Persian king Xerxes. He is referred to in Ezra 4:4-7. During this time the enemies of Israel hired counselors to bring false accusations to the ears of the different Persian kings. They are listed, at least as it seems, in chronological dating order. First to Cyrus, then to Darius, then to Ahasuerus, then to Artaxerxes. The Persian king who ruled between Darius and Artaxerxes was King Xerxes.

The interesting thing about Xerxes was that he did indeed rule from India to Ethiopia and this is verified from an inscription from the Persian ruler himself which states: "King Xerxes says: . . . "the countries of which I was king apart from Persia. I had lordship over them. They bore me tribute. What was said to them by me, that they did. My law, that upheld them: Media, Elam . . . India . . . and the Nubians (Ethiopia)."

In the beginning of the book of Esther, Ahasuerus invited all the rulers of his kingdom to come to the city of Shushan (Susa) to behold Persia's glorious palace.

This palace was constructed mainly by his father Darius who brought the best craftsman from all the nations under his rule to build it. One of Darius's inscriptions reveals it's majesty:

"This palace which I built at Susa, from afar its furnishings were brought . . . The cedar timber from the mountains of Lebanon. The Assyrians brought it to Babylon; from Babylon the Carians and the Ionians brought it to Susa . . . The gold was brought from Sardis and from Bactria . . . Precious stones were brought . . .

The silver and the ebony were brought from Egypt. The ornamentation with which the wall was adorned came from Ionia. The ivory which was carved here was brought from Ethiopia . . . The stone columns were brought from Elam. The stone-cutters were Ionians and Sardians.

The goldsmiths were Medes and Egyptians. The men who fashioned the wood were Sardians and Egyptians. The men who made the baked bricks were Babylonians. The men who adorned the walls were Medes and Egyptians.

Darius the King says: "At Susa a very excellent work was ordered and a very excellent work was accomplished."

Another inscription from Xerxes says that He carried on the work at Susa after his father's death. It states: "Much that is beautiful that my father Darius built . . . I added to and erected additional construction."

A similar inscription from Susa states: "King Xerxes says: I built this palace after I became King."

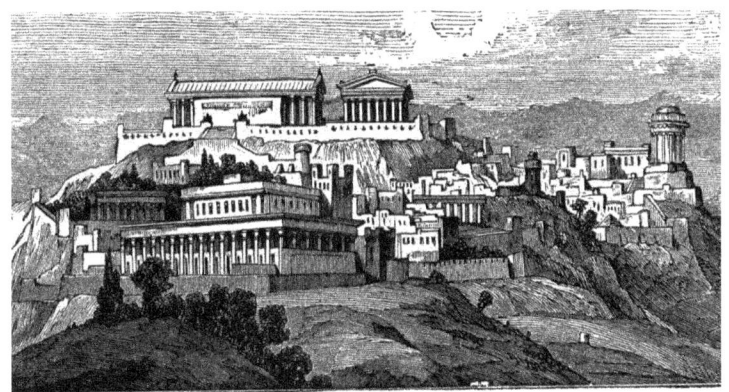

ANCIENT SUSA.

To get an idea of how magnificent Susa was, when Alexander the Great destroyed the city later on in history, the historian Plutarch accounted that the wealth taken from Susa amounted to 40,000 talents of coined money and other furniture and untold wealth. And just as much was found at Persepolis as found in Susa. He also wrote that it took ten thousand pairs of mules and five thousand camels just to carry away its wealth.

Another historian, Diodorus Siculus, said that the treasuries at Susa included 40,000 talents of silver along with 9,000 talents of gold darics.

Xerxes also had a grandfather by the name of Hystapes also known as Vishtaspa. This Vishtaspa did have some ruling authority under Cyrus, as well as alongside his son Darius who was the father of Xerxes. And the interesting thing about his name is that it sounds very similar to Vashti, the disobedient queen mentioned in the book of Esther. Could Vashti of the book of Esther be referring to the Queen of Vishtaspa?

Not much is known about Vishtaspa's wife. But Vishtaspa's death along with one of his wives is recorded in history as follows:

"Darius ordered a tomb to be built for himself in a two-peaked mountain, but when he desired to go and see it, he was dissuaded by the soothsayers and his parents. The latter, however, were anxious to make the ascent to it, but the priests who were dragging them up, being frightened at the sight of some snakes, let go the ropes and they fell and were dashed to pieces. Darius was greatly grieved and ordered the heads of the forty men who were responsible to be cut off."

It may be possible that Xerxes married Vishtaspa's daughter, in other words princess Vishtaspa. But this is only speculation.

As to records of Mordecai and Esther, the ancient historian Ctesias may record them in his writings as follow:

"Darius was succeeded by his son Xerxes . . . His other confidential advisers were the aged Mardonius and Matacas (Mordecai?) the eunuch."

Ctesias continues: "Xerxes married Amestris [am-ESTR-is] (Esther?) . . . Xerxes, then crossed over into Asia and advanced towards Sardes, dispatched Megabyzus (his son in-law) to plunder the temple at Delphi. On his refusing to go, the eunuch Matacas (Mordecai?) was sent in his place, to insult Apollo and plunder the temple. Having carried out his orders he returned to Xerxes, who had arrived in

Persia from Babylon."

There are other Persian artifacts that may indeed refer to Mordecai as well. They are known as the Persepolis Treasury Tablets documented by the University of Chicago's Oriental Institute.

The first artifact is dated to the 32nd year of Darius, just four years before Xerxes begins his rule. It states:

". . . In the 32nd year . . . Hipirukka wrote, the receipt from Marduukka he received" (Marduukka being very similar in pronunciation to Mordecai)

The second artifact is dated to the 7th year of Xerxes, just four years after the account in Esther. It states:

". . . the woodworkers and relief makers which Marduka-nasir sent" (Again, the first part of this man's name "Marduka" sounds very similar in pronunciation to Mordecai.)

The third name which is found on a variety of different Persian tablets and are dated to the third year of Xerxes, the exact year of the Esther narrative, is "Irdakaia." And on one of these tablets, two other men mentioned in Esther 1:14, Tarshish and Meres may also be listed. The Inscription reads:

". . . Tarkauish (Tarshish?) says . . . silver to workmen . . . earning wages at Parsa, whom Mauis (Meres?) is responsible . . . Laborers at the columned hall . . . 3rd year (of Xerxes) . . . Receipt from Irdakaia (Mordecai?)

Another letter written in the 6th year of Xerxes may also mention Carcas, a servant of Xerxes, mentioned in Esther 1:10. It states:

" . . . silver to them give . . . whom Mauis (Meres?) Is responsible . . . Of the columned hall . . . 6th year (of Xerxes) a sealed order has been given. Karkiis (Carcas?) wrote, the receipt of which Irdakaia (Mordecai?) received."

As to Esther, both the historians Herodotus and Ctesias record that the queen of Xerxes was named Amestris (am-ESTR-is), which contains the word Esther. And both historians record that she held great power and influence during the reign of her husband Xerxes as well as that of her son Artaxerxes. For example, Ctesias records that Amestris was given authority by the king a few times which allowed her to give orders to execute and punish the enemies of her family. During one incident she commanded that certain men captured in battle, who were responsible for killing her son Achaemenides, were to be executed. She also had the man responsible for killing her grandson executed as well.

This is similar in fashion to her actions in Esther 9:13 where she asks the king that the ten sons of her enemy Haman be hanged because they tried to exterminate her people.

According to Ctesias, she also interceded to spare the life of her innocent son in-law Megabyzus who had saved her son Artaxerxes from being mauled by a lion. Similar once again in fashion to her intercession with king Xerxes to save her people from an edict by the king that would have destroyed them all.

WHO WILL INTERCEDE FOR YOU WHEN YOU SIN AGAINST GOD?

"If one man sins against another, God will judge him. But if a man sins against the LORD, who will intercede for him?" 1 Samuel 2:25

"Who is he who condemns? It is Christ who died, and furthermore is also risen, who is even at the right hand of God, who also makes intercession for us." Romans 8:34

My righteous Servant shall justify many, For He shall bear their iniquities . . . Because He poured out His soul unto death, And He was numbered with the transgressors, And He bore the sin of many, And made intercession for the transgressors.

Isaiah 53:11-12

Therefore He is also able to save to the uttermost those who come to God through Him (Jesus Christ), since He always lives to make intercession for them. Hebrews 7:25

If you have enjoyed this book, please pass it along to a friend. Jesus said "Freely you have received, freely give."

May the Grace and Peace of the Lord Jesus Christ be with you.

This book as well as our first and third volumes in the Bible Believer's Archaeology series may be ordered at BibleHistory.net as well as from other major online book distributors.

SOURCES:

THE HOLY BIBLE, AUTHOR: THE LORD GOD
Scripture taken from the New King James Version unless noted.

The author and publisher gratefully acknowledges the following resources used in compiling data and illustrations for this publication.

FRONT COVER: Artwork: "Christ Presented to the People"
Illustrated in "Durch Ganz Italien" (1923), author Schumman's Verlag

GOD'S GREATEST GIFT: Art: "The face of Jesus"
Illustration © copyright 1997 John Argubright

CHAPTER #1: "KINGS OF THE EAST SHALL BOW"

Tacitus, Histories 5.13 mentions that the Jews believed the Scriptures contained a prophecy that when the East was powerful a ruler would come forth out of Judea to secure a universal Empire.

The Lives of the Caesars - Life of Vespasian 4.5 says a belief was held all over the Orient that a ruler would arise out of Judea and establish a government over all men.

(Testament of Judah 24.1-6)
The Testament of Judah was part of a collection of texts supposedly written by the twelve sons of Jacob known as The Testaments of the Twelve Patriarchs.
Fragments of two of the Testaments have been found in the Dead Sea Scrolls, those of Levi and Naphtali, the former in Aramaic, the latter in Hebrew.
Oriental Institute - University of Chicago Carbon 14 dating chart: Shows "Testament of Levi" as dated between 100-200 B.C. from the "Annals New York Academy of Sciences, Vol 722, pg. 446
http://www-oi.uchicago.edu/OI/PROJ/SCR/DSS_Chicago_2000/DSS_Chart.html (2003)

Photographs of Dead sea scroll fragments of Testaments of Naphtali, Judah, Benjamin, Jacob, Joseph. and Levi.
http://www.deadseascrolls.org.il (Explore the Archive under Parabiblical Texts)

Sheba is located in present day Yeman, southern Arabia. Midian is located in northwest Arabia on the eastern side of the Gulf of Aqaba. Dedan located in south east Arabia, present day Oman.

Song: We Three Kings. Author and Composer John Henry Hopkins Jr.

Artwork: "Three kings bow before the Messiah" Illustrated in Pilgrim's Progress (The Illustrated Family Bunyan) with Introductory Essay on the Life and Writings and Genius of the Author by the Reverend W. Landels) circa 1880. Publisher: James Sangster & Company.

CHAPTER #2: "BY HIS STRIPES"

Mishna; Pesahim 8:6 gives reference to the custom of releasing a prisoner during Passover.

Philo, In Flaccum, book 36 gives the account of how the Alexandrians mocked a man as the king of the Jews.

Josephus, Jewish War, Book 2: chapter 14: 9
Account of Florus method of crucifixion and scourging.

Artwork: "Men blindfolding and mocking Christ" Illustrated in "Ageless Story" (1939), Author: Lauren Ford.

Artwork: "Roman soldiers scourging Jesus" Illustrated in "Art and Music" - ChildCraft Vol.13" (1939) Publisher: "Quarrie Corp.

CHAPTER #3: "SERGIUS PAULUS"

Journal of Theological Studies, NS, Vol 56, Pt 1, April 2005 (Article from oxfordjournals.org) Article name: "Possible Inscriptional Attestation to Sergius Paulus (Acts 13:6-12), and the implications for Pauline Chronology."

"Some Archaeological Observations on Paul's First Missionary Journey," Author: Bastian Van Elderen, W.Ward Gasque & Ralph P. Martin, eds., Apostolic History and the Gospel. Biblical and Historical Essays Presented to F.F. Bruce. Exeter: The Paternoster Press, 1970. Hbk. ISBN: 085364098X.pp.150-161.
Chapter 9: information on Sergius Paulus inscriptions.
http://www.biblicalstudies.org.uk/pdf/archaeology_vanelderen.pdf. (2006)

First Cyprus Inscription from Soli — Inscriptiones Graecae ad res Romanas pertinentes III.930. Corrected reading in T. B. Mitford, Annual of British School at Athens 42 (1947) pp. 201-06.

Second Cyprus Inscription from Kythraia - Inscriptiones Graecae ad res Romanas pertinentes III.935. John L. Myers translation, Handbook of the Cesnola Collection of Antiquities from Cyprus (New York: Metropolitan Museum of Art, 1914), p. 319 (no. 1903) and p. 548 (no. 1903).

Inscription 3 from Rome mentioning L. Sergius Paulus as a curator of the Tiber river — GIL VI.3 1545.

Cyprus: Its Ancient Cities, Tombs and Temples. 1878 pg424 Louis P. di Cesnola

Archaeology and Bible History, Author: J.P. Free
pg. 269 Ramsay found the name Lucius Sergius Paulus in 1912 at Pisidian Antioch (Yalvac Museum).

C. Plinius Secundus *The Historie of the World.* Book II. (Pages 1-49) Philemon Holland, translator (1601):
Pliny the elder lived between 23-79 A.D. and when finished with his work on History of the World dedicated it to the emperor Titus in 77 A.D.

C. Plinius Secundus *The Historie of the World.*
Book 30:11: Latin "est et alia magices factio a Mose et Janne et Lotape ac Iudaeis pendens, sed multis milibus annorum post Zoroastren, tanto recentior est Cypria."

Devia Cyprus (notes on an archaeological journey in Cyprus in 1888) D.G. Hogarth, pgs.110-115

Inscription bearing the name L. Sergius Paullus as curator of the Tiber river in the reign of Claudius. www.yorku.ca/uhistory/courses/4131/sources/caput_xiii.htm (July 2006): CIL06, 31545 (p 3796, 4362) = D05926

Artwork: Pen and Ink reproduction of the Quintus Sergius Paulus inscription based upon photo of artifact. Illustration © copyright 2007 John Argubright.

Artwork: Pen an Ink reproduction of the L.Sergius Paulus inscription based upon photo of the artifact located at the Yalvac Museum at Pisidian Antioch. Illustration © copyright 2007 John Argubright.

CHAPTER #4: THE SAMARITAN TEMPLE"

Josephus The Essential Writings, ISBN 0-8254-2963-3, Author: Paul Maier
P197-200: How the Samaritan Temple was Built by Sanballat for Manasseh and the account of Alexander the Great's experience in Jerusalem.
P221 Hycranus attacked the Samaritans who were allied with the Macedonians and destroyed the temple at Gerizim.

Coin from Jaddua the high priest.
http://fontes.lstc.edu/~rklein/images2/jaddu.JPG (2011)

Article: "A silver coin of Yohanan" (Pls II-V) L.S. Fried
Coins from Jaddua the high priest, and his father Johanan, both mentioned in Nehemiah 12:11. A coin of John Hycranus has been found as well.

Donation for the Samaritan Temple full inscription:
"The Israelites of Delos, who donate to the temple of Mt. Gerizim, crown with a golden crown Sarapion, son of Jason, from Knossos on account of the benefaction towards them" Discovered in 1982 Hanson dates 150-50 B.C. others date 250-175 B.C. If dated after the temple was destroyed it would have shown that the Samaritans continued to worship on mount Gerizim even without a temple.
http://www.kchanson.com/ancdocs/greek/samben.html (2011)

Artwork: "Samaritan woman speaking to Jesus at Jacob's well" Illustrated in "The New Testament - A Pictorial Archive from Nineteeth-Century Sources - 311 Copyright-Free Illustrations" Edited by Don Rice, Publisher: Dover Publications.

Artwork: "Alexander the Great kneeling before the Jewish High Priest." Artist: Casper Luyken (circa 1700 A.D.)

CHAPTER #5: "ACTS 17 - THE UNKNOWN GOD"

In 1820 an inscription was found on Palatine Hill : "Whether to a god or goddess / Sacred C Sextius/son of Praetor C.F. Calvinus/ by order of the senate/ has restored it" http://en.wikipedia.org/wiki/Si_deus_si_dea (2009)

"They fashioned a tomb for thee. O holy and high one. The Cretens, always liars, evil beasts, idle bellies. But thou art not dead, thou livest and abidest forever. For in thee we live and move and have our being." Epimenides Cretica approx. 600 B.C. http://en.wikipedia.org/wiki/Epimenides_paradox (2009)
"The Cretens, always liars,evil beasts, idle bellies." Also quoted by Paul in Titus 1:12

Aratus "Phaenomena 1-5": "Let us begin with Zeus, whom we mortals never leave unspoken. For every street, every marketplace is filled with Zeus. Even the sea and

the harbors are full of his deity. Everywhere, everyone is indebted to Zeus. For we are indeed his offspring.
http://spindleworks.com/library/rfaber/aratus.htm (2009)
Aratus (315-240 B.C.), also Cleanthes (331-333) stated "we are his offspring."
http://www.soniclight.com/constable/notes/pdf/acts.pdf (2009)

"The Book of Acts" F.F Bruce ISBN 0-0828-2505-2 pg.336 Diogenes Laurtius, who tells (Lives of Philosophers 1.110) how the Athenians once, during a pestilence, sent for Epimenides, a wise man of Crete (C. 600 B.C.) Who advised them to release black and white sheep from the Areopagus and then, on the spot where each lay down, to build and sacrifice on that altar the sheep. He also stated that "Anonymous altars (altars to unnamed gods) might be seen throughout all Attica."

The Lives and Opinions of Eminent Philosophers by Diogenes Laertius, Translated by C.D. Yonge Book1. "Life of Epimendes" Paragraph III Epimendes Account of Athenian altars built without names as memorials to the sacrifice during the plague to appease the unknown God.
Http://classicpersuasion.org/pw/diogenes/dlepimenides.htm (2009)

Book Title: A People for His Name - A Church Bases Missions Strategy by Paul A. Beals pg 32 also http://www.wikinfo.org/index.php/Epimenides:
Diogenes Laurtius : "Altars may be found all over Attica which have no names inscribed upon them, which are left as memorials to the atonement."
Pausanius "Description of Greece vol 1, 1:4" as well as Philostratus "Appolonius of Tyana" both refer to "altars to an unknown god."

Artwork: "The Unknown God" Illustrated in "Chambers Encyclopedia - Vol.9 (1875) Author J.B. Lippencott.

Artwork: "Palatine Hill Inscription" mentioning "To a god or goddess" based upon photo. Illustration © copyright 2009 John Argubright.

Artwork: "Sacrifice on an Altar" Illustrated in "Bermuda" book published prior to 1946 by author Ethel and Catherine F. Tucker, Publisher Pillans and Wilson. (1911)

CHAPTER #6: "BERNICE AND HEROD AGRIPPA II"

Banias, The Story of Caesarea, Author: John F Wilson.
Note 70: Translation of the Beirut Inscription.

Women in Scripture, Authors Meyers, Craven, Shepard, Kraemer.
Pg. 59-60 Photograph of the Beirut artifact mentioning Bernice and Agrippa. Note: Bernice is as mentioned on a statue in Athens that honors her as a "great Queen".

The Building Program of Herod the Great 1998
Author: Roller, Page 249 a drawing of the Beirut Inscription.
Page 250 (The actual Inscription reads)
"R]egina Berenice Regis Magni A["
"Qu]od Rex Herodes Proavos Eorum Fecerat Ve["
"Marmor [ ]que Et Columnis [S]ex"

Argubright's translation used Perseus Latin Morphological Analysis word study available at: www.perseus.tufts.edu/cgi-bin/morphindex?lang=la
Literal Translation:
Regina="Queen", Berenice="Bernice", Regis = "King or ruler", Magni="magnificent

or great", A[....] assumed to be Agrippa possibly referring to King Agrippa I, Bernices father, but most likely King Agrippa II her brother and great grandson of Herod, Quo="who with respect to", Rex="king", Herodes="Herod", Proavos from proavus = "great grandfather", eorum = "their, he or she", Fecerat from facio = "construct or build", Marmor = "marbles", [ ]que=? Inscription not clear, Et = "as well as", Columnis= "columns or pillars", [S]ex= "the number six".

The Book of Acts by author Frederick Bruce
pg. 451, note 27: on a Latin inscription from Beirut she is called "Queen Bernice, daughter of the Great King Agrippa the first ..." Comptes rendus de 1' Academie de Inscriptions" (1927) pg 243-244
On a Greek inscription in Athens she is called "Julia Berenice, the great queen" (IG III.556 = CIG 361)

Artwork: "The Conversion of Paul" Artist:Henry Felix Emmanual Philippoteaux, Illustrated in Cassell's Illuminated Family Bible Vol. 4 from Matthew to Revelation pg.201, Publisher: Cassell, Petter & Calpin (1860).

Artwork: "Paul before Herod Agrippa", Artist: H.Anelay & W.J.Lintom, Illustrated in Cassell's Illuminated Family Bible Vol. 4 from Matthew to Revelation pg.229, Publisher: Cassell, Petter & Calpin (1860).

Artwork: "Beirut inscription mentioning Bernice and Agrippa" based upon photo: Illustration © copyright 2008 John Argubright.

Artwork: "The Resurrected Christ rising the Dead" Illustrated in "Anyone can Draw!" (1939) Author: Arthur Zaidenberg, Publisher: World Publishing.

CHAPTER #7: "THE FINAL SCAPEGOAT IS CHOSEN"

Talmud, Rosh HaShanah 31b, & Bavli, Yoma 39b:
the scarlet cord quit turning white the last 40 years the Temple was standing.

Artwork: "The High Priest laying the sins of the people onto the scapegoat" Artist: William James Webb (19 th century)

Artwork: "The scapegoat by artist Holman Hunt" Illustrated in "Virgil Aenid" (1944) by author John Dryden. Publisher: Heritage Press.

Inscribed on the frame of Holman Hunt's artwork: "Surely he hath borne our Griefs, and carried our Sorrows/Yet we did esteem him stricken, smitten of GOD, and afflicted.' (Isaiah 53:4) 'And the Goat shall bear upon him all their iniquities unto a Land not inhabited.' (Leviticus 16:22)
    This was Hunt's first major painting made during his first stay in the Holy Land. Hunt's researches disclosed that on the Festival of the Day of Atonement, a goat was ejected from the temple with a scarlet piece of woolen cloth on its head. It was goaded and driven, either to death or into the wilderness, carrying with it the sins of the congregation. It was held that if these sins were forgiven the scarlet cloth would turn white. Hunt regarded the Old Testament scapegoat as a prefigurement of the New Testament Christ whose suffering and death similarly expunged man's sins. In the Book of Leviticus (which is quoted on the frame) the goat is said to bear the iniquities into a land that was not inhabited. Hunt chose to set his goat in a landscape of quite hideous desolation - it is the shore of the Dead Sea at Osdoom with the mountains of Edom in the distance. In his diary Hunt described this setting as 'a scene of beautifully arranged horrible wilderness 'and he saw the Dead Sea as

a 'horrible figure of sin', believing as did many at this time that it was the original site of the city of Sodom. (Liverpool Museum)

CHAPTER #8: EXODUS FROM THE PYRAMIDS"

Exodus: The Route-Sea Crossing-God's Mountain by author G.M. Matheny ISBN 9781613792971 Publisher Xulonpress.
Pg. 69 Philo and Eusebius have Moses at Memphis.
Pg. 75 Succoth believed to be Saqqara cemetery near Memphis.
pg,137-138 Baal-Zephon = "Lord of the North" believed to be the protector of mariners.
Pg.102 Herodotus quote of Delta becomes like a sea and passes near the Pyramids.
Pg .150 Herodotus quote of Nile becomes like a sea.

Ancient Near Eastern Texts Relating to the Old Testament - James Pritchard.
Egyptian Texts mentioning the Sphinx. ANET 449 (Thutmose IV), ANET 244 (Amenhotep II), ANET 366, ANET 368, ANET 371-372.
ANET 252 - Tutankhamun mentions being in the palace of Thutmose I which "note 5" says from another inscription seems to have been at Memphis.

The Golden King, The World of Tutankhamun. Chapter 2, The Golden Age pg24 Author: Egyptologist Zawi Hawass. Amenhotep II Built a temple at Giza, dedicated to the Great Sphinx as the sun god HoHoremakhet (Horus in the Horizon). The Memphite desert was very important as a training ground for young princes: and near the area of the Sphinx was known as the Valley of Gazelles.

Ancient Records of Egypt, The Eighteenth Dynasty, Author: James Breasted 1906 Volume 2 - The University of Chicago Press.
Pg. 321 Inscription, found on a monument near the Sphinx, mentions Amenmose who was the first born son of Thutmose I (the likely Exodus Pharaoh). The inscription reads: "In the fourth year of his majesty Thutmose I, beloved of **Harmakhis (the Sphinx)** . . . The eldest king's son, commander in chief of his fathers army, Amenmose, living forever took a pleasure walk."
Pg.428 Inscription from Pharaoh Eye (Ay or Aye) mentions Thutmose I palace at Memphis: "King Aye, while he was in Memphis. His majesty granted him the lands as a reward . . . the north is the "House of Ptah" and the "House of Okheperkere." (Thutmose I)

Eusebius of Caesarea: Praeparatio Evengelica (Preperation for the Gospels) (1903) Book 9 Translation by E.H.Gifford.
Account of Moses at Memphis.

Greek Septuagint, Genesis 46:28-29 identifies Goshen with Heroopolis (Hermopolis), Exodus 1:11 adds the third city of Heliopolis (On) to the cities of Rameses and Pithom.

Memphis is (Men-nefer) in Egyptian, in Greek it was known as Hut-ka-Ptah (enclosure of Ptah)

http://en.wikipedia.org/wiki/Sekhmet (2012): Sekhmet also is a solar deity, sometimes called the daughter of the sun god Ra. Sekhmet was believed to protect the pharaoh in battle, An early Egyptian sun deity also, her body was said to take on the bright glare of the midday.
http://en.wikipedia.org/wiki/Mount_Aqraa (2012): Lord of the North information.

""http://henadology.wordpress.com/theology/netjeru/sekhmet/ (2012): "The pharaoh is sometimes characterized as "brother [*sen*]/image [*senen*] of Nefertum, born of Sekhmet."

http://www.catchpenny.org/seconds.html The Arab writers who mention a 2nd Sphinx are: Al-I'Drisi (AD 1099-1166) who wrote about it in *Kitab al-Mamalik wa al-Mansalik* (a large geographic encyclopedia) and *Al-Kitab al-Jujari*, a geographical encyclopedia on Asia and Africa. He describes a second sphinx across the Nile from the first in a very bad state of repair, made of mud (bricks) and faced with stone, most of the stone having been hauled away by local inhabitants and now the Nile "lapping at its feet." He doesn't say if it was the same size, but since the Nile moved further east after AD 1166, then it would have been destroyed.

Ibn Battuta (AD 1307-1377) in his *Travels in Asia and Africa* doesn't mention it, either because it doesn't exist, or had already been destroyed by then (it was written around AD 1325-1354).

Musabbihi mentions a smaller Sphinx across the Nile from the large one "south of Cairo" in a "ruined state of brick and stone" in the *Annals of Rabi II* around AD 1024 Nasir-i Khosrau visited Egypt between Aug 1047 and April 1048 and heard rumors of a second one. Msftedit 5.41.15.1507

Stepped Pyramid at Saqqara, http://en.wikipedia.org/wiki/Pyramid_of_Djoser (2012).

Sekhemkhet's unfinished complex at Saqqara near where three kings built their pyramids. http://www.ancient-egypt.org/index.html (2012).

Artwork: "Egyptian Pyramids and Sphinx" Illustrated in "Library of Universal History Vol 01" (1898), Author: Clare, Israel Smith, Publisher: Union Book Co

Artwork: "Sphinx of Egypt" Illustrated in "Travels Around the World" (1873) Author: Seward, W. Publisher: Appleton Co.

Artwork: "Pharaoh's chariot" Illustrated in "The Book of Histories Vol.5," The Grolier Society. (1915) Pg.2113

CHAPTER #9: "THE BOIL PLAGUE ON EGYPT"

Article: "Evidence of the Exodus, Scars from the Plague of Boils" Author; Ed Kaspar. (2009) http://www.biblehistory.net/Exodus_Evidence.pdf

Discovery Channel video "Secrets of Egypt's Lost Queen."
Cat scans of Thutmose II, Hatshepsut, Sitre-In, and Thutmoses III.

Analysis of 4 possible Exodus scenarios (Matching 2 proposed Biblical time lines against 2 Commonly used Egyptian Pharaoh time lines)
http://www.biblehistory.net/Exodus_Date.pdf

Josephus The Essential Writings, Author: Paul Maier,
pg. 48 pharaoh's daughter named "ther-muthis"
pg. 49-50 Moses battle in Ethiopia and his Ethiopian wife

Inscription of Ameni account of famine during Sesostris I reign.
http://reshafim.org.il/ad/egypt/texts/ameni.htm (2009).

Artwork: "The Plague of Boils" Illustrated in "Histoirie de L'Aeronautique" (1938) Author: Charles & Bouche, Henry Dollfus.

Artwork: "Pharaoh's daughter drawing Moses from the water" Illustrated in "The Child Bible being a consecutive Arrangement of the Bible" (1884). Author: Dr. J.H. Vincent, Publisher: Castle and Company.

Artwork: "Mummy of Thutmoses II: Illustrated in "The Book of History - Volume 5" pg. 2069 Publisher: The Grolier Society.

CHAPTER #10: "ISRAEL AND THE HEBREWS"

www.bible.ca - Merneptah stele - Israel section translation.

http://en.wikipedia/wiki/Merneptah_Stele (2009).
In 1896 Flinders Petrie located the stele at Thebes. The stela size is roughly 10 feet in height by 5 feet wide and is dated to 5th year of Merneptah (1209-1208 BC).

Ancient Near Eastern Texts - Relating to the Old Testament.
Author: James Pritchard:
ANET 276-278 - Merneptah Stele mentions Israel.
ANET 22 - Thutmose III taking of Joppa, Mention of the "Apir."
ANET 246 - "List of his booty: . . . Canaanites: 640."
ANET 247 - "List of the plunder which his majesty carried off: Princes of Retenu (Syria): 127, Brothers of princes: 179, Apiru: 3600 , Shasu (Bedouin): 15,200."
ANET 254(a) states: "Year 1 . . . the foe belonging to the Shasu are plotting rebellion.
ANET 254 states: "foe belonging to Shasu from the fortress of Sile to the Canaan."
ANET 255 " states: "The Apiru of Mount Yarmuta with Teyer have risen in attack upon the Asaiatics of Rehem." Yarmuta is Biblical Jarmuth.
ANET 242 Thutmose III inscription, list "Jacob-EL", and "Joseph-EL.."
ANET 243 Rameses III inscription mentions "Levi-El."
ANET 487 "May the king, my lord, know that the chief of the Apiru (Hebrew) has besieged the lands . . . it is only I and Abdu-Heba who fight against the 'Apiru (Hebrew) chief." Amarna letter #RA xix p.106.
ANET 259 mentions the "Shasu (Bedouin) tribes of Edom", (reference Pritchard - Footnote 2.
ANET 262 - The Egyptians called the Edomites (the descendants of Israel's brother Esau) the "Shasu of Edom."
Summary of the Northern wars from Ramese III says: "I destroyed the people of Seir (main territory of the Edomites) among the Shasu (Bedouin tribes).
http://www.archaeowiki.org/Topographical_List,_First_Campaign_of_Thutmose_III

Actual List from Thutmose III Listing "Jacob-El" and "Joseph-El."
Egypt, Trunk of the Tree By Simson Najovits, pg. 179-180:
Topographical List from Karnak.
Thutmoses III - Jacob-el, Joseph El, Shasu Springs.
Rameses II - Jacob-el, Joseph-el.
Rameses III - Jacob-el, Joseph-el, Levi-El, Asher.

The Shasu of Yahweh source:
Amenhotep III - 1386-1349 BC. Topographical List - 1386 BC. In the temple of Amon in Soleb there is a topographical list from the time of Amenhotep III (1408-1372 BC). In column IV. A2 is written" ssw yhw" which means "Yahweh of the land of the Shasu" (Giveon 1964, 244; Redford 1992, 272; Astour 1979, 17-34). In the ancient Near East a divine name was also was given to a geographical place where the god was worshiped (Axelsson 1987, 60). This is the first clear extra-biblical evidence of the name "Yahweh."

One name in the mentioned lists from Soleb and Amarah in Nubia Sudan - 'Yhw (in) the land of the Shasu.'
Shasu of Yahweh is a term that appears in Egyptian inscriptions of the 18th and 19th Dynasties (c. 1540-1190 B.C.). One, found at Amarah or Amrah in Upper Nubia, dates to the reign of Seti I (c. 1300 B.C.). An earlier inscription, probably from the reign of Amenhotep III (c. 1400 B.C.) was found at the Temple of Amun in Soleb, Sudan.

Artwork: "Merneptah inscription mentioning "Israel, the foreign people" based upon photo. Illustration © copyright 2009 John Argubright.

Artwork: "Inscription mentioning "Shasu of Yaweh" based upon photo" Illustration © copyright 2009 John Argubright.

CHAPTER #11: "JOASH KING OF SAMARIA"

Ancient Near Eastern Texts Relating to the Old Testament Princeton University Press 1969 Edited by James Pritchard   ISBN 0-691-03503-2.
ANET 655 - Zakir of Hamath Stela text mentioning Benhadad, the son of Hazael, king of Aram.
ANET 282 -Sabaa Stela Mentions Adadnirari III attack on Damascus and tribute paid.

http://referenceworks.brillonline.com: Calah Orthostat Slab (2.114G) Adadnirari III march against Omri land (Israel) and Damascus and tribute paid.

http://referenceworks.brillonline.com: Sabaa Stela (2.114E) Mentions Adadnirari III attack on Damascus and tribute paid.

http://referenceworks.brillonline.com: Tell Al Rimah Stela (2.114F) Adad-Nirari III's artifact mentioning Joash.

http://fontes.lstc.edu/~rklein/images5/zakkur.jpg = photo of Zakir Stela which mentions Ben-Hadad and Hazael.

Artwork: "Joash shooting an arrow" Illustrated in "American Portraits" (1946) Author: Fisher, Dorothy Canfield, Illustrator: Kaufman, Enit   Publisher: Henry Holt and Co.

Photo: "Tell Al Rimah Stela mentioning Joash" published on the website http://en.wikipedia.org/wiki/File:Adad-Nirari_stela.jpg - listed as Public Domain, with notice This work is in the public domain in the United States because it is a work prepared by an officer or employee of the United States Government as part of that person's official duties under the terms of Title 17, Chapter 1, Section 105 of the US Code. US Department of State posted as stolen from the Iraq National Museum.

CHAPTER #12: "MENAHEM"

Ancient Near Eastern Texts - Relating to the Old Testament. James Pritchard, 3rd Edition, Princeton University Pres 1969 ,
Pg.283 Account of Menahem's tribute to Tiglath- Pileser III and the Assyrian kings statement that he left Samaria alone.

Halley's Bible Handbook ISBN 0-310-25720-4
pg.195 Menahem's reign (748-738 B.C.).

Iran Stele Inscription - from Tiglath-Pileser III Text and Photograph.
http://ochre.lib.uchicago.edu/zincirli/index_files/Page928.htm (2010).

Iran Stele Inscription photograph and text.
http://www.english.imjnet.org.il/htmls/popup.aspx?c0=13152&bsp=13055 (2010).

Tiglalth Pileaser COS 2.117A. COS 2.117B.
http://fontes.lstc.edu/~rklein/Documents/Assins.htm#Tiglath.

ANET/COS Cross reference charts.
http://fontes.lstc.edu/~rklein/Doc5/COS-ANET%20Index.htm. (2010)
http://www.bombaxo.com/cosanet.pdf.

Iran Stele - Israel Museum Info.
http://cojs.org/cojswiki/Iran_Stele,_737_BCE (2010).

Josephus Antiquities of the Jews 9:228-236   William Whiston, A.M., Ed.

Avigad's comprehensive Corpus of West Semitic Stamp Seals (WSSS 35) Hami'ohel seal - Seal: "Belonging to Hami'ohel daughter of Menahem". The seal was found in Jerusalem and is dated to the seventh century. Its center is decorated with fish and fins and a long tail.
Women in Ugarit and Israel: their social and religious position, By Hennie J. Marsman pg.646   Seal: "Belonging to Hami'ohel daughter of Menahem."

http://www.bib-arch.org/debates/seal-controversy-06.asp (2010).
Hami'ohel daughter of Menahem - Proven provenced wsss35.

Artwork: "Tiglath Pileser" from the walls of his palace artifact located in the British Museum. Bible View Clipart 4.0, copyright © 1998 Pastoral Computer Services.

Artwork: "Iran Stele" based upon photos.
Illustration copyright © 2010 John Argubright.

CHAPTER #13: "TIRHAKAH"

Ancient Near Eastern Texts Relating to the Old Testament Princeton University Press 1969 Edited by James Pritchard. ISBN 0-691-03503-2.
Anet 288 - Epigraph from a relief depicting the conquest of Lachish at the palace of Sennacherib.
Anet 287 - From the Nimrud Inscription which mentions Sargon II victory over Judah and Hamath.
Anet 532 - The British Museum text 79-7-8,195 - Artifact from the reign of Ashurnirari V mentions Arpad as being subject to Assyria.
Anet 301-302 - The Babylonian Chronicle in the British Museum mentions Sippar and Akkad being taken by Sennacherib and appointing his son Ashurnadinshumi as ruler over them. (Sippar and Akkad being associated with Sepharvaim.
Anet 292 - From the British Museum text K3082+S2027+K3086 from the reign of Esarhaddon which mentions Ba'lu, king of Tyre who trusted Tirhakah king of Nubia to defend him.
Anet 290 - Esarhaddon Text mentions his capture of Tyre who put his trust in Tirhakah king of Nubia.
Anet 293- From the Senjirli Stela mentions Esarhaddon's campaign against Memphis and his wounding in battle of Tirhakah.

Anet 294-295 - Rassam Cylinder of Ashurbanapal's first campaign against Tirhakah, also mentions how the Necho dynasty started.
Anet 294 A list of kings subject to Assyria is listed on Cylinder C. They include Manasseh king of Judah.
Anet 291 - The Esarhaddon Col. 5 - "I called up the kings of the country Hatti and on the other side of the river (Euphrates) Ba'lu king of Tyre, Manasseh king of Judah Registration # 1929, 1012.1.
Anet 303 - The Esarhaddon Chronicle 627 B.C.
"First year of Shamashshumukin (king of Babylon, brother of Ashurbanapal) - The army of Assyria marched against Egypt, Tirhakah king of Egypt . . , the country of Egypt . . . Necho [king of] Egypt.
Anet 281 The Calah Slab mentions Adadnirari III putting many countries under his rule including Israel. Two other inscriptions, the Tell Sheik Hammad Stela as well as the Orthostat Slab mention Adadnirari's defeat of Arpad.

The Bible in the British Museum - Interpreting the Evidence. Author T.C. Mitchell. ISBN: 0-8091-4292-0
pg. 76 Document 35 Tablet fragment from Shalmaneser mentions Assyrian titles of Tartan and Rabshakeh. ANE 82-5-22. 526.
Pg. 77 Document 36 Bilingual clay label dated to 645 B.C. makes mention of the title Rabsaris. ANE 81-2-4, 147.

Tell Sheik Hammad Stela British Museum #131124
Mentions the conquest of Arpad as follows:
"Atarsumki [from Arpad and the kings] of the land of Hatti who had rebelled . . . In a single year, I conquered the land of Hatti."

Orthostat Slab also mentions Arpad's conquest.
Atars[umki ...] trusted [in his own strength, attacked to wage war and battle. I decisively defeated him. I took away his camp. [...] the treasure of [his pal]ace [I carried off.]

Artwork: "Bas Relief Siege of Lachish by Sennacherib" Illustrated in "Popular and Critical Bible Encyclopedia Vol. 2 (1910).
Author: S. Fallow, Publisher: Howard-Severance Co.

Artwork: "Rassam Cylinder: Illustrated in "Popular and Critical Bible Encyclopedia - Vol.1" (1910). Pg.180 Author: S. Fallows, Publisher: Howard-Severance Co.

Artwork: "Senjirli Stela from Esarhaddon located at the Pergamon Museum mentions Tirhakah", Illustrated in 'Book of History Volume 4 (The Near East Section) pg.1680, publisher: Grolier Society.

Tirhakah article Internet sources (2012) :
http://en.wikipedia.org/wiki/Arpad_(Syria)
http://en.wikipedia.org/wiki/Sepharvaim
http://classic.net.bible.org/dictionary.php?word=SEPHARVAIM
http://en.wikipedia.org/wiki/Tirhakah#Biblical_references

CHAPTER #14: "JOSIAH'S BATTLE WITH NECHO"

Ancient Near Eastern Texts Relating to the Old Testament - Princeton University Press 1969 Edited by James Pritchard. ISBN 0-691-03503-2
Anet 304-305 - In the fourteenth year of Nabopolasar (612 B.C.) - The fall of Nineveh and Ashuruballit becomes the new Assyrian king ruling out of Harran
Anet 305 - In the Sixteenth year of Nabopolasar (610 B.C.) his forces along with the

Manda-hordes attack Ashuruballit at Harran and the Assyrian king flees.
Anet 305- In the Seventeenth year of Nabopolasar (609 B.C.) Ashuruballit's army combined with Pharaoh Necho II's army and try unsuccessfully to try and take back Harran.

www.livius.org/cg-cm/chronicles/abc2/early-nabopolassar.html: (2013)
Babylonian Chronicle (ABC 2) - BM 25127 (98-2-16, 181)
Early years of Nabopolasar and his defeat of the Assyrians at Babylon.

www.livius.org/ne-nn/nineveh/nineveh02.html (2013)
Babylonian Chronicle (ABC 3) - BM 21901 ((96-4-9, 6)
Fall of Ninevah, Assurballit becomes Assyrian king and he and Egyptians forces combine to battle the Akkadians at Harran.

www.livius.org/cg-cm/chronicles/abc4/late-nabopolassar.html (2013)
Babylonian Chronicle (ABC 4) - BM 22047 (96-4-9, 152)
Army of Egypt in the twentieth year of Nabopolasar (606 B.C.) stationed at Carchemish crossed over the Euphrates and made the army of Akkad withdraw.

www.livius.org/cg-cm/chronicles/abc5/jerusalem.html (2013) (BM 21946)
Babylonian Chronicle (Jerusalem Chronicle) (ABC5) Reign of Nebuchadnezzar: The defeat of the Assyrians and Egyptians at the Battle of Carchemish 605 B.C.

Artwork: "Egyptian Warrior on Chariot," Illustrated in Library of Universal History - Volume 1, Author: Israel Smith Clare. Publisher: Union Book Co. (1898).

CHAPTER #15: "JEREMIAH - CHAPTER 39"

Biblical Archaeology Review Nov/Dec 2007 Page 18.
Article "Cuneiform Tablet Confirms Biblical name" in regards to Nebo-Sarsekim.

Ancient Near Eastern Texts Relating to the Old Testament.
Edited by James Pritchard ISBN: 0-691-03503-2
ANET 307-308 The Court of Nebuchadnezzar prism found in Babylon mentions Nebuzaradan and Nergal-Sharezer.

History of Ancient Israel and Judah, Author: James Maxwell Miller (1986).
pg. 422 Photograph of seal "Gedaliah who is over the House."

Westminster John Knox Trust - The Welcome Trust.
Photograph of seal "Gedaliah who is over the House."

Artwork: "Judean king being led into captivity" Illustrated in: "Art and Music- Childcraft Vol. 13" (1939) Publisher: Quarrie Corp.

Artwork: "Seal of Gedaliah who is over the House."
Illustration copyright © 2013 John Argubright.

CHAPTER #16: "DANIEL AND THE CIA AGENT"

Dead Sea Scrolls Deception By Michael Baigent, Richard Leigh pg.10-11 Story of Miles Copeland and the Daniel Scroll.

Dare to be a Daniel by Author David Hocking Promise Publishing ISBN 0-939497-20-3, 0-939497-26-3 pg. VI In Daniel the grammar goes "subject, object and verb in the sentences. In the Dead Sea Scrolls it goes subject, verb and object."

Apologetic Press - Reason and Revelation - April 1995 The Dead Sea Scrolls and Biblical Integrity by Gary K. Brantley, Article regarding the authenticity of the Book of Daniel http://www.apologeticspress.org/articles/266 (2011)

Tyndale Bible Dictionary -Walter A. Elwell, Philip Wesley Comfort pg.352 - 90 percent of the Aramaic words used in Daniel were used in the Old and Imperial Aramaic dialects.

http://www.schoyencollection.com/HebrewAramaic.html (2011)
Photos of the Daniel scroll fragments "MS 1926/4" with the text of Daniel 3:22 - 31.

Artwork: "Egyptian kneeling holding a scroll" Illustrated in "Scribners Monthly-Vol. 11" (1876), Author: Scribner and Company, Publisher: Francis Hart & Co.

CHAPTER #17: "ESTHER AND MORDECAI"

Astyages ruled from 585-550 BC. (According to the Greek historian Herodotus.) In order to fit the book of Esther which takes place in the third year of Ahasuerus, if Astyages was the king it would be 583 B.C.

Astyages - Akkadian name - Istumegu.
http://www.livius.org/as-at/astyages/astyages.htm (2011)

Josephus - The Essential Writings by Paul Maier.
pg.115 The Historian Josephus states that Astyages was the father of Darius the Mede. Jewish Antiquities X.249.

Xenophon's Cyropaedia states that Cyaxares II followed Astyages to the throne of Media and whose brother was Mandane. He was the uncle of Cyrus, and he cooperated with Cyrus to conquer Babylon. http://en.wikipedia.org/wiki/Cyaxares_II

Neo-Babylonian Texts in the Oriental Institute Collection by David B. Weisberg. The University of Chicago. Oriental Institute Publications. Volume 122, Text 38. Mentions Nergalsumibni son of Marduka (Mordecai?) Who lived in the first year of Cyrus and Darius the Mede.
http://oi.uchicago.edu/OI/DEPT/PUB/SRC/OIP/122/OIP122.pdf (2011)

Archaemenid Royal Inscription XPh from Persepolis.
Known as the "Daiva Inscription" Archaeological Museum Tehran Inscription from Xerxes stating he ruled to the borders of Ethiopia and India.
http://www.livius.org/aa-ac/achaemenians/XPh.html (2011)

Archaemenid Royal Inscription Xsc from Susa.
"King Xerxes says: I built this palace after I became King."
http://www.livius.org/aa-ac/achaemenians/XSc.html (2011)

Ctesias Persica #19 - Photius recorded an excerpt from Ctesias Persica #19 where Darius parents died visiting his tomb being carved into a mountainside. They died approx. 495 B.C. Darius father's name was Hystapes also known as Vishtaspa.

Persepolis Treasury Tablets by George C. Cameron - The University of Chicago. Oriental Institute Publications. Volume LXV (65)
http://oi.uchicago.edu/pdf/oip65.pdf (2011)
oi.uchicago.edu/OI/DEPT/PUB/SRC/OIP/65/OIP65.html

pg.10-11 Account of Susa's wealth captured by Alexander the Great as recorded by Plutarch - Alexander 36-37 Loeb & Diodorus Siculus Xvii. 66
pg.16 Account of Xerxes continuing the building projects.
Note 104 pg 13 History of Herodotus III - Herodotus IX, 107 f
Herodotus stated that the Persian kings divided their year between Babylon, Susa, Ecbatanna (probably Persepolis as well in the case of Xerxes.)
    pg. 83-84 (Text 1) mentions a man named Marduukka (Mordecai?) In the 32nd year of Darius of Persia.
    pg.125-127 (Text 25) Mentions "... woodworkers and relief makers Marduka-nasir (Mordecai?) sent" Dated to the 7th year of Xerxes.
    pg.110-112 (Text 15)   Mentions "... Tarkauish (Tarshish?) says ... silver to workmen ... earning wages at Parsa, whom Mauis (Meres?) ... laborers at the columned hall ... 3rd year (of Xerxes) ... Receipt from Irdakaia (Mordecai?)
    pg.120-123 (Text 22) "... silver to them give ... whom Mauis (Meres?) Is responsible ... Of the columned hall ... 6th year (of Xerxes) a sealed order has been given. Karkiis (Carcas?) wrote, the receipt of Irdakaia (Mordecai?) he received."

Photius Excerpt of Ctesias - Persica 1 (24-32)
Mention of Matacas (Mordecai?) And Xerxes wife Amestris (am-ESTR-is) Esther?
http://www.livius.org/ct-cz/ctesias/photius_persica2.html (2011)

Artwork: "Xerxes Coin" Illustrated in The Book of History a History of All Nations From the Earliest Times to the Present (Volume V The Near East The Hebrew Peoples, Persia, Arabia, Asia Minor, Heroic Age of Islam, Egypt, V The Near East (1915) by The Grolier Society. Printed by The Colonial Press. PG.1813

Artwork: "Ancient site of Susa" Illustrated in "History of the World Vol. 1" (1909), Author: Ridpath, J. C., Publisher: Jones Brothers Publishing Co.

Artwork: "Persian King with armor bearer and advisor" Illustrated in "Library of Universal History Vol 01" (1898), Author: Clare, Israel Smith., Publisher: Union Book Co.

Notes: If Kish was taken captive to Babylon at lets say 20 years of age in 597 B.C. at the time of Jehoiachin's captivity. Lets say at age 30 he became the father of Shimei (587 B.C.), Lets assume Shimei became the father of Jair at age 30 (557 B.C.), and Jair fathered Mordecai at age 30 (527 B.C.) Then in the third year of Xerxes 484 B.C. Mordecai would have been around 43 years of age. Speculating the same for Artaxerxes the first whose third year of reign was 463B.C., Mordecai would have been 64 years old. Speculating the same for Artaxerxes II, whose third year was 402 B.C. Mordecai would have been 125 years old which means he was probably dead by this time. If Mordecai's ancestors averaged fathering sons in the line lets say at the age of 25 then Mordecai would have been 58 at the time of Xerxes and 79 at the time of Artaxerxes. So it appears that Xerxes is the most reasonable candidate if these assumptions are true.

Some believe Artaxerxes I was the Ahasuerus of Esther, for example Josephus in his Antiquities of the Jews as well as the Greek Septuagint identifies him as Artaxerxes. The problem with this is that Ezra 4:6-7 clearly distinguishes that Ahasuerus and Artaxerxes are two different kings, and their names are spelled differently in Hebrew.

Some believe that Artaxerxes II was also known as Ahasuerus
http://en.wikipedia.org/wiki/Artaxerxes_II_of_Persia
But there a couple of problems with this view, First in order for Mordecai to have

been alive at this time, his great grandfather, grandfather, and father all had to have been in their fifties at the time their sons were born and Mordecai would have been advanced in years at the time of the book of Esther.

Secondly, Egypt led a successful revolt against Persia and became independent in 405 BC, therefore it is highly unlikely Artaxerxes II whose third year would have been 403 B.C. could have made the claim his borders extended to Ethiopia as Esther 1:3 states. Although he did build a palace at Susa as found on the following inscription.: A2Sd - Inscription on Column base from Susa states:

'I am Artaxerxes, the great king, the kings' king, king of all nations, king of this world, the son of king Darius, the Achaemenid. King Artaxerxes says: By the grace of Ahuramazda, I built this palace, which I have built in my lifetime as a pleasant retreat." http://www.livius.org/aa-ac/achaemenians/A2Sd.html (2011)

REAR COVER: Illustration: Partial reproduction of the crucifixion from Rembrandt's "The two criminals" Artist: Rembrandt.

www.ingramcontent.com/pod-product-compliance
Lightning Source LLC
Chambersburg PA
CBHW051452290426
44109CB00016B/1727